About the Author

Madame Kapuscinska is quite the unpredictable randomer who enjoys a quiet life with fun, joy, and laughter. She's hypersensitive and a deep thinker who always wonders, *What if she could have been that bit better within to make a difference?* She's quite a loner who's often misunderstood; friendships are quite difficult for her. The closest to her are her family, her children, and her husband; they are her rock; they don't judge her and love her imperfectly for being her.

Restored

Madame Kapuscinska

Restored

Vanguard Press

VANGUARD PAPERBACK

© Copyright 2024
Madame Kapuscinska

The right of Madame Kapuscinska to be identified as author of
this work has been asserted by her in accordance with the
Copyright, Designs and Patents Act 1988.

All Rights Reserved

No reproduction, copy or transmission of this publication
may be made without written permission.
No paragraph of this publication may be reproduced,
copied or transmitted save with the written permission of the publisher, or in
accordance with the provisions
of the Copyright Act 1956 (as amended).

Any person who commits any unauthorised act in relation to this publication
may be liable to criminal prosecution and civil claims for damages.

A CIP catalogue record for this title is available from the British Library.

ISBN 978-1-83794-337-1

This is a work of nonfiction. No names have been changed, no characters
invented, no events fabricated.

*Vanguard Press is an imprint of
Pegasus Elliot Mackenzie Publishers Ltd.*
www.pegasuspublishers.com

First Published in 2024

**Vanguard Press
Sheraton House Castle Park
Cambridge England**

Printed & Bound in Great Britain

Dedication

To my husband, who has continuously supported me with my bipolar disorder, and to my children, for their strength and courage in understanding such a condition at such a young age. My mother for raising me single-handedly, and my Uncle Michael for our many long discussions.

Acknowledgements

I would like to acknowledge all the people who have crossed my paths on this journey of life and the many patients who inspire me. I would like to acknowledge Sarah and Nigel for enabling me to land my dream job as an oncology complementary therapist. It's been the greatest opportunity.

Synopsis

This book is about how a young black female diagnosed with bipolar effective disorder, ADHD, severe dyslexia, and fibromyalgia turns her life around through her own regime of natural health. It explores the many obstacles she faced and struggles she overcame daily to sustain a more balanced well-being. Taking into consideration her spiritual beliefs and experiences of past traumas, betrayal, deception, and the general stigma and difficulty that come with having mental health. Eventually, she was accepted by the doctors to respect her wishes in how she wishes to manage her health through the use of complementary therapy.

For many years, Duchess Letitia has fought through trialling many different medications to find that all she would experience would be the negative side effects, which would give her new symptoms that she was experiencing. She turns her obstacles into creativity by recognising earlier that the very best way to progress and enable change is to implement the changes within. Looking within herself, this meant looking at how her relationship is with her family— a mother or two with sons who have autism and ADHD and a supportive husband who stands by her.

Duchess Letitia further goes on to explore her entrepreneurship skills and tools that individuals can incorporate through self-reflections and affirmations. Because it generally starts with changing your mindset and taking yourself outside of your own comfort zone. In the society we live in today, mental health is on the rise. Very often, individuals are a part of many people's lives through the expansion of digital technology and the world of social media. Your day-to-day posts of memes and what you do in your day-to-day life impact others without you even realising it. Quite often, people are losing sight of the importance of human interactions and what it is like to talk face-to-face with an individual, as it is very much zoom, FaceTime, and video calls. We have continued the isolation that was born through the digital era, and we are becoming unable to understand the communication that is often not spoken. When a person speaks to you in person, quite often, what is understood is the mannerism in which it is spoken, their body language in how they deliver it, and then, slightly, the actual context of what is given.

This book tries to align many different factors that affect one from being whole and living their best life fully. It touches upon how one can uplift oneself and sustain that upliftment through constant self-learning. Life is lifelong learning, and different circumstances and situations in life are about new parts of ourselves that we have yet to discover for ourselves. Duchess Letitia has a way of connecting with her readers in the way she writes. It is captivating as a musical artist, and writing also comes second nature.

This book will help you reach deeper levels of understanding of yourself because of the very person you are so attuned to.

Biography

Duchess Letitia Kapuscinska is a senior oncology complementary therapist at HCA in Harley Street, London, UK, and author of *My Mind's Eye: See You Soon Angel*. She is also known for her make-up line and gym wear line.

Letitia Antoinette is a reverend and award-winning artist known as Madame Kapuscinska and Letitia Kapuscinska, born in Luton. She is a professional international singer, songwriter, actress and model. Her family originates from St. Lucia and Guyana; she is based in North London.

At the age of sixteen, Letitia moved onto government work. She was representing the east of England as a young advisor in regeneration and renewal. She got to meet Princess Anne and worked with Andy Burnham, Ed Balls, Tessa Jowell, and Hazel Blears, all within different departments of the government. she has also done a documentary for 'Black History Month'.

Life has thrown all sorts of twists and turns at her, but despite the challenging past, Letitia Kapuscinska has remained victorious. She is among those individuals who battle with fibromyalgia and bipolar disorder. But as a complementary therapist, she does her best to heal naturally through self-love, self-care, and fighting the fears and worries of what-ifs. She wants to empower people to discover who they really are, to fight their fears, and to go above and beyond in living their best lives now and being in this moment, releasing the past, and turning their pain into creativity. Letitia has endured heartaches through sexual abuse and kidnapping in the past. It does not define her, but it became a part of who she is today—a strong woman who works hard and never gives up. She draws art from her pain. Her trauma is reflected in her work.

Change

I wish I could sleep; it's like 2.05 a.m., and still, my mind won't rest. Really and truly, what is bothering me? Why am I so anxious about what is bothering me? Lol. I am at peace, I guess, and it feels so loud; it's scary, lol. I am so not used to it. It has been a long time coming. Those I needed around have been around, and those I no longer need have no sounds. Strange coincidences. When you start doing good in life and are so aligned, not everyone is happy for you, and those who genuinely love and care for you celebrate your successes, sometimes just waiting in anticipation for when their time is coming when it is actually happening at the same time as it's happening to you. Alignments mean all that is connected, as we are all one. Everyone is minding their business, and so are you, so don't get to worry about what others are doing. How often do you see a sprinter looking back to see where the competitors are? They are staying on track in their lane as you fast as a lightening baby. So, it is time to be proud of where you are and delighted about where you're going and how you're landing. The Lord has chosen you to rise and wake up today. It is good that you listen to the signals and signs; just be more positive with the mind, and yes, you will go through the negatives, oh, so briefly of accord to just hear the ins and outs of what passed. As the saying goes, "Tread your water carefully." Sometimes, take your steps cautiously, but as for good luck, break a leg while you are at it. Now, I don't want you to literally do that, so, you know, wear comfortable footwear for where you need to go. Your wisdom is beyond you most of the time. Even your present self does not always get where you are coming from, but you are blessed to be blessed. Stay blessed, don't stress, and just take little tests. You are the horizon, so shine brightly. They see you coming from miles away, and your love is spreading like fog. Because when God is working, you can't always see what He is working on. Maybe you can feel the breeze, so breathe easy, deeply, and slowly.

I came to a point in life. Where enough is enough, it is time for change; it's time for healing; it's time for reconnecting, believing in oneself, and restoring faith in hope, love, and dreams.

I decided to clean up my way of life. Starting with how I think, how to not think of the people who hurt me in the past or of past relationships that no longer exist. I started to stop my mind from going over the past choices and decisions that were once made because that time has passed and is in the past. I decided to reflect on what healthy relationships are. How do I truly feel amongst some people? Is it good? Is it natural? Is it forced? Am I not truly myself? Am I uncomfortable? Are the conversations one-sided? Do they actually respond to you when you say something that requires a kind of investigative nature as to why you have feelings about it? Do they ignore it or bother? Because healthy friendships and relationships are supportive of a bridge, which enables you to continue to be free-flowing and not place a block. I decided to stop smoking and get back to exercising. I decided to try to get my fitness back up and jog around the area. I decided to stop certain hobbies, such as singing, and replace them with the normalities of life and a better routine. In this society of lockdown, it is the norm not to have to leave the house to earn money now that it naturally isolates you from the real world out there as much of it is becoming virtual. Nonetheless, the usual nine to five is a craved normality that requires you to leave the house and have interaction with humans. I started cooking more often. Healthier routines are returning. Definitely a lot of TVs, but easily replaced with activity once well persuaded without incentive.

So I got called in to help support my staff today, as we had two sick members at reception. The manager told me this rarely happens. My thoughts were that there's nothing like being thrown in the deep end when new to a position and getting stuck in to learn the ropes of the way. To be fair, it is in drastic situations that I tend to thrive, so there is nothing like putting myself to the test. To see, I still got it. I also got to speak to a dear friend who's also going through changes. New work, new homes. Changes are occurring everywhere, every day, in every way. It is such a blessing when you notice the positivity of the changes, yet we rarely tend to see the blessings when it may feel as though they seem negative. That could be a blessing because in the negatives is actually where the deep digging occurs of realisations of situations and whose there and whose not and the how's and why's to things. Those are different types of processes that cannot always be so easy to endure, even if they are positive. If everything were ever so easy, would we truly appreciate the gift that's to be received? I am not too sure because we always notice and resonate with others; some don't resonate, and that is the thing about change.

We learn to respond differently, and we develop new ways to digest and absorb new information. We may integrate old with new for balanced views. I had a change of perspective on the way I've been viewing myself. I took a trip down memory lane with the doctor as we went through the procedure of investigation as to whether or not I had ADHD. Yes, I've spent a lot of time analysing myself, my behaviour, and my ways of life, and I've even been able to suspect the possibilities and years of education to deem it suitable to somehow manage to self-refer myself to this. Little did I know that I was presenting signs of ADHD at an early age. It's not a requirement to be diagnosed, but sometimes something just changes in you, and you want to understand further why you do the things you do or why you tend to attract certain different personality traits or relationships in your life. There are always different factors that drive an action or way of doing things. So changes are unanimous in reality because, just as the seconds, minutes, hours, days, months, and years pass, we are ever-changing and growing in all that we do. Sometimes, we fail to realise that because we are hard on ourselves and unable to recognise the actual efforts that we put into our day-to-day lives. I mean, getting up out of bed, washing your body, and brushing your teeth are all processes of change. Not everyone has the possibility to be able to do these things themselves, so it is exactly, as I mentioned earlier, a blessing to have the capability of change, whether it be negative or positive. Something deeper is always going on, and it has an adverse reaction to the world around you, even if you're not moving. The changes in your life have effects all around. We are divinely connected, even through the nothings of the day.

There are so many changes occurring at once in a whirlwind of speed that one truly has no idea whether they are coming or going. But they know they must keep moving forward; there is no turning back. There is no time to go backward. It is OK to go over a redo better than the last, but it can be overwhelming.

There is no telling how things will turn out, but one must think positively about the outcomes. Most times, to others, you're doing much better than you think of yourself, so it appears effortlessly, even though you may be so knackered underneath it all.

Our ways of life and views of life are ever-changing because of the things we experience. Be it a loss, a trauma, or a change of good luck, an appreciation sinks deep to the core because I believe it is always worth trying to be better and do better.

So, how was your Tuesday? My Tuesday was tepid and strange. I mean, I learned skills within my new role and started researching the necessities to start my new role. Then I enjoyed the new skills for my current role. A proper choice is Tuesday, then top it off with work drinks with the staff after work. I was so happy, a little tipsy, that I had to leave as I still had the kids to put to sleep when I got in. But what did I notice as I was getting ready to inform you of my day? A missed call from the new role. Then, what was I thinking before I boarded the train? I am starting to like it here; it is going to be difficult to leave. Goodness me, choices on a Tuesday; could it happen on any other day than choosey Tuesday? Not at all; I say divine timing. Divine timing can be so scary when it always comes in time. You know what I mean. Oh, how I do give myself a headache with the predicaments that I place myself in. But I guess that's my own way of always giving myself choices, yet I am an indecisive type. I get so connected with clothes and things that I talk to the items when shopping as to which one I should pick. Will you make me feel good? What difference will you make in my life? Oh damn. What do I do? Laugh, I say, and go with the flow. Today, I told my friend she has to stand up and voice her opinions if she wants to see the change. She said she couldn't when it was family. I forgot to tell her right now that it's family vs. family when your own bubba ain't well and you're not well, but one must go to work for family because it doesn't make a difference to speak. In this case, it was her actions that spoke louder. Pretty much the same as me. I mean, how did I truly feel among the team? I felt grateful to be away from work and grateful to be amongst people. I am grateful for the invite. But did you get into the personality? Hmm, one question to herself: I guess I did, and I didn't. Well, I didn't talk much. I hated when attention came to me to talk, as I am generally used to others talking amongst themselves in social situations; that is the autism side of me. I prefer to observe. I really don't know. Part of me was still digesting the invitation and being in place amongst others. I think I am such a strange being at times that I can't see much about myself that is worth talking about. But when I think about the things I'm into and do, I guess I still have that one-on-one person situation, but at most times I prefer for the other to break the ice. Because I guess in certain roles, depending on how you learned and conditioned your mind, you naturally see your manager as like a parent, someone you're looking up to, and you kinda want to be in their good books. Especially when you are starting a new position. But I am in a position where I may be leaving, and I get so quick to see everyone as friends, as I truly do believe we are all brothers and sisters at the end of the day. Hmmm. I do frustrate myself with my thinking. I think I had too much of a drink. You know what I'll do as I get off the tube at the next four stops? I'm going to make that call to Grace. I mean, I am a duchess; I am usually meant to be addressed as your Grace. But to have Grace as the name of the person who is kinda, like the leading person of the foreseen future. I really view her as the saving grace, the amazing grace, just like in the church hymn. There's a blessing in disguise there that I can't fully understand, but I definitely feel like she is the route of the blessing, even though it takes me to take a role. Interesting and fascinating to see. I wanted to invite my manager to my birthday doo, but another part was to hesitant because I saw a Tik Tok video about a work colleague. I am just trigger-happy all day, every day, but not literally all day. Because I complain half the day, all the day, and most of the way till I'm satisfied, then convince myself it is all right. What can I say? I was my own worst enemy and my own best friend at the time. Be content with yourself. I say it helps you think clearly. But what makes you feel content? Hmm, hmmm. Things go according to plan, but what is the plan when you believe there is a God upstairs laying things out right before you that you have already subconsciously chosen? Damn, you chose We are still on Choose Day, and it is such a strange one.

God is taking your bitterness and making something sweet. Life feels so uniquely strange. This whole adjustment to change just leaves me flabbergasted in a good way. I haven't experienced this way of life before, and I guess I feel like I am dreaming because it is so great. I do not know how to talk about it, but I write. My husband's happier; my children behave even better; and there's less stress and drama around me. I guess this is what my peace is like. Work is great, and my colleagues are so supportive.

So I am back again to the changes chapter, and I tell you, it really does take a while to adjust to changes. My current changes in adjusting are a new job, new daily routines, new gym habits, and the maintenance of motivation to train. Roles as a mother ensure kids get their homework completed and in bed at an earlier time. Starting a new handbag line means keeping in touch with manufacturers and logistics. Starting a new business, I thought I'd join the utility warehouse to schedule times to do quotes. Change, change, changes everlasting. Change is in progress, and the thing that tops it off is just having that belief mindset that one can achieve many things if they are dedicated and mindful of the ever-changing roles that one has. Not just that, but to be mindful not to overdo it so as to have balance along the way.

So, this week has been a new change for me. I've been attending the gym earlier in the morning to go to exercise classes. Before, I was a person who did't do early mornings, but to change, one must be the change. My mind feels clearer, I have more energy, and, to be fair, managing stress is much better. I got home after my session and pressed my doorbell, waiting for my husband to open the door. He didn't answer. I pressed it a second time. Then, third, I just called him in case he couldn't hear it from where he was. The old me would have been irritated, banging on the door. I even acknowledged to myself that, wow, I handled that well. I responded in a calming manner because you never know what someone is doing while you're waiting. I felt quite proud of myself for that. Even in my exercise class today, I struggled, but when you look in the mirror, it is like, come on, you can do this. You need to be strong and fit for this future self of yours that is forming right before you.

So many changes have been occurring in my life due to a changed mindset. Feeling stronger in oneself. Taking time to meditate and exercise. Taking time for self-care, taking time to relax. I tell ya, I did some Hatha yoga today, and I felt renewed, strengthened, hopeful, energised, and fruitful. Life is opening up to me in a new way. Giving me newfound confidence is amazing. The difference is in applying yourself to your life in a dedicated, positive way. If everyone could try to change the way they look at themselves and life, many things could change miraculously for you. I went to go for a blood test today, and the doctor had no belief in herself that she'd be able to get my blood. She apologised and apologised nonstop. Before even attempting, I had told her I felt awesome. I just finished yoga, and she said, "Oh well, it's all in the mind." As she struggled, I told her to try to get blood from my fist. She was so hesitant. Little did we know, she managed to get some. I told her it was all in her mind, and she laughed. But it is true that people can tell you positive words but then dismiss them and not even apply them to themselves. So be mindful of the things that come out of others and be more focused on what is true to you.

Well, hello there. I return again to chapter change. I mean, it could go on forever, just the concept of change because we are ever-evolving. So, I spent the bulk of last week in recovery from my new gym regime of training and attending exercise classes. It seems it took its toll on me. I had no idea how energy-draining it could be. I was shattered. I cancelled four out of seven exercise classes and was so heavy on myself. I felt so terrible for not going. I was telling myself that I wasn't going to keep up the momentum of change. But little did I care to realise and acknowledge that change actually takes patience; change is a process in which you adapt, you adjust, you grow, you strengthen, you build, your body regenerates, your body heals, your body repairs. The most important part of change is the recovery of change. Actually, we are the change because we are the change. My change required a detox cleanse of mind, body, and soul. I reweaned myself from smoking and actually had a dedicated day for this. My last smoke let me enjoy the goodbye of the lessons it has taught me. Be it the experiences, good or bad, it is important to be able to healthily digest and acknowledge that not all processes may have been as pleasant as we are ever learning from life itself. So I returned to training today thinking, let's attempt some new classes this week as we are still finding our way. What type of training works best for you? Being bipolar, I quite often experience mood swings, so I kinda get bored quickly from sessions if they are overly repetitive in that they remain the same each week. That has been my experience so far. So, I will attempt some new classes this week and then get on with designing my own programme that works best for me. Apart from my sense that I may have anger built up, I got the boxing gloves ordered. I have not yet attempted boxing. I think the first thing in the morning is a great time to train, especially before the kids are awake. It seems I am most alert these times, so I can use that to push myself a bit more. I noticed I don't like to be motivated by others. It winds me up as if I am not training hard enough. I much prefer pushing myself in my own space with self-satisfaction. I am aware of what works and what does not. Last week was a lot of negative chatter because of the foreign feeling of change, but I understand I need to rest in order to be able to return and continue. It could be one day, a few hours, or a few days a week. For me, it was a few days, and so much negativity built up subconsciously that it was like training it all away and letting it go through each effort of training. It's quite a psychological process to rebuild yourself, for sure. But it was all worth it in the long run. Do things for yourself first because it feels good and makes you feel good for yourself. Not for others first.

Getting myself fit is going to give me more energy in the long run, less stress, more productivity, and more feeling good within myself. My feeling better about myself has a positive outcome for my family and my children.

Journeys

I do find it hilarious the journeys to work. You observe and see so much without realising it. The young generation that still rocks with half the backside showing through the trousers cracks me up because, by the time they leave the train to try to get to their next destination, they are busy pulling up their trousers so they can walk properly and just wear them properly in the first place. Goodness knows what truly is proper any more, just like it is normal nowadays. All those things are kinda on the boring side. So what is happening on the tube this morning of my fascinating journey of the day? Majority are on their phones, a few are with their headphones listening to God knows what, some are reading the paper, and quite a few are staring into space of the day. Thinking, contemplating, and wondering how their day is going to be. I was thinking, should I of done that? Was that the right choice? Some have sadness in their eyes. Where is my life truly going? Some have defence in their eyes, like, why the heck are you looking at me? Another is wondering why and how I am still alive. There are not too many glimpses of joy, but then I see one person with a gentle smirk as he texts away. I really don't know what reception they have under here on the underground. I guess we all would rather our eyes be busy doing something than capture the lock of another set of eyes opposite us. Because what do we say to strangers in the morning when they are crowded and still waking up for the day? I just passed Caledonian Road and need to get to Holborn. I'm hoping I get to my changing station in good time on my second day of work; I don't want to be running late. It does feel strange in a good way to have a new position. I feel like it is necessary to have to take some work home so you can check what the day ahead is looking like. King Cross St. Pancras is such a busy stop. Everyone who has joined the tube can now hardly move. I'm grateful for my chair. I wouldn't really think of myself as much as an author or writer, but I guess that is exactly what it is: writing the thoughts that come to your mind and having them in some kind of patterned flow that keeps a reader reading, you know, what I mean. Oh, that is nearly me. One more stop to go. I think I will be arriving at the perfect time—no, not just perfect. I predict I will, as the options and time are showing strongly that it is a good possibility. I was even trying to, but it was the intention that mattered that helped me get on my way. Positive vibes and a positive mind. I enjoy this way of thinking; it seems more healthy and clearer.

So Holborn is just a busy station in the morning to change into. I get out, tryna do my change to the central line. Feeling a rush of anxiety, my heart is beating so fast out of my chest, along with a sense of excitement about the day being amongst the rush of people and the eagerness of the journey to be somewhere on time. Amongst possibly like-minded people striving and trying to achieve it, just going with the assumption that the majority are on their way to work, to study, to the hospital, to help someone, to visit someone, to get up to mischief. Whichever it is there on the motion of doing. The doing is what helps us be productive and get things done in our day, but yeah, rest assured, as I sit, the heart is still bumping like crazy because those sounds of the tube get me differently. Journeying on the tube isn't anything of relaxing but stimulating in a strange way of curiosity and anxiousness, praying nothing goes strong whilst on the journey to a to z. Sometimes, it is easy to drive away from the focus of what you are trying to obtain while you get occupied with other things. It is important to bring yourself back to the centre. One more stop to go. Like I said, I will arrive in good time. I could have gotten away with not walking up the escalators, but I guess I feel the need to get to the loo, too. Why is that also the case when travelling? It's not like I was drinking along the way to get here; guess that coffee I had this morning has run its course. I feel so tired. Time for a top-up, I think. The hustle and bustle of just trying to survive is just so trying at times. I mean the survival of being able to afford a roof over ya head, food in your belly, kids, and household clothing with heat and energy to supply the premises. Whether you have a disability or not. But mine is with me, both physically and mentally. Trying to return to a stage you once were at by trying to allow your body years to recover, recuperate, and heal and realising that the only way to heal and recover is to get back into action. So, talking in terms of being self-employed, when you're trained in a trade that doesn't make your condition better physically but mentally, it keeps you more stable. Yet life seems to have so many hiccups that make it difficult for you to appear reliable to others. But on the other flip of the coin, because it is a hustle, while one door may not be fully working, the others are opening and still sailing through OK in a sense, and without realising it, you were actually paving the next path of your self-employed path with your control while one door closed. I try to work at least a day in a clinic treating people with manual therapies, and the other days in and out of care homes providing treatment for those less able to move; ask me which one I prefer. Much prefer both, but you can't have both when life is pulling you elsewhere and your cabin at home awaits for you to do your own treatments. Travelling sure causes way too much anxiety, and the workload is so much at times that it is difficult to stand. Yet, for yourself in your own space, you have more choice and freedom to state when enough is enough. I think I got kindly let off today without the let off as I'm still useful on standby should someone not turn up, but at the same time, standby works better in not having to commit as one does prefer her own space of time without being ordered. Then, on the other side of the coin, your

YouTube account has finally gotten enough subscribers that it's at that stage to start generating income. Even if it is only a few pence for now, it is still a start, and we have to start somewhere. Even if, on the other side of the coin, you're a post supervisor on a film and a music director and songwriter and have songs to write and a que sheet to prepare, it's going on a schedule that you're just waiting for feedback and approval to move forward with your team. Even the morning started with an offer for an interview about how a wife and mother manage running a business by themselves and any tips or pointers as to how to help others. I thought about that question to myself: how would I answer the truth? It's all God. God fills me with love, joy, and hope that even on my darkest days, I somehow go on. He told me to plant my seeds long ago, and many say don't put your eggs in too many baskets. I may not have as many kids as the eggs lay comfortably in my womb; however, my eggs have tended to be my skill set, talents, and entrepreneurial flair that I have to hold on to. That tends to be my harvest, and I guess my bipolar conditions kind of keep me up and down, so I always listen to what I feel is good for me. I hold God deep in my heart because I believe God is love, and in my life, I do quite believe that the meaning of names is important and is part of your purpose in life. Mine means to bring joy beyond praise. I don't believe that means I must just bring joy beyond praise into others' lives, but I believe I must know how to apply that joy beyond praise in my own life first.

To me, first, that means utilising all the gifts that I've been blessed with in the best way possible to fulfil me. By knowing how to do that, I will positively do my best to teach my family how to do so, too.

Early morning, 9.17 a.m., on the underground. I got up at six a.m., returned to sleep, rose at seven a.m., and had some fried eggs, grilled cheese, and toast with a cappuccino. It felt good to have the strength to prepare some breakfast to have strength and energy for the day ahead. This means some improvements are in process in preparation to be able to partake in the day. Some don't have the luxury of being able to get themselves up independently. I sure struggle and am incapable of doing so on my worst days. So I'm really grateful for today. I pray it's a great day. Full of wonders and miraculous surprises. God knows I endure and favour them. You never truly know what to say at times when you're writing. I write and go with the flow of what comes to me. Of what feels right. It feels right to live and make the most of this day, as much as I may be battling with my health and my body to stay up and focused. I can do it if I really try. Last night, I felt the urge to call around a few sisterly friends to check in on them as I took them under my wing with distant healing, so I have felt obliged to ensure that they are also keeping their lives in order and fighting to keep upright and happy as much as the obstacles they may be fighting I to have my own so it's a duty to ensure that I do my best to overcome them. I believe I am. I may not be able to see it, but I feel it within.

It has been four months now without medication for the mind. So, my body has been adjusting and repairing itself. I experienced many setbacks, as you know. With health issues, you can have one thing wrong or many things wrong, and at times, medication can either make another illness worse, bring about new symptoms, or even improve things. I had new symptoms, and things were getting worse. It was ridiculous, really. I think it was a clear sign that the medication was not the right one for me.

When I find that medication is not working, I return to the route of alternative medicine, which starts with what I am digesting into my body. What foods are good, and what social interactions are healthy? How am I responding to situational causes? I reflect to improve, and other times, I'll break down and cry or wallow in self-pity, then further into depression and further into the physical capabilities of my body, just giving up. It is a tiring but unfortunate cycle, but sometimes, well, most times, cycles are purely to help you learn about yourself.

Day of operation: umbilical. It's been a long time since I gave in to surgery after being advised otherwise. I sit, waiting patiently. I Just saw the anaesthetist, who's advised I may be sick afterwards. I will be knocked out and prescribed morphine. I think morphine how I've missed this dear friend. I've literally had a deeper relationship with medication than I do with people. How deep a pain it can reach vs. how much one can cause to you.

Nurses are laughing, and doctors are smiling. There are positive vibes in this ward. Better doctors are happy than miserable when operating, I think. Happiness brings out that passion even more than the love of the job. Worried I am of the after-effects. Will my throat hurt? If only I could record this experience. I am always curious about what goes on when one is put to sleep now. But no, I shall go to La La Land; think positive thoughts. That maybe maybe maybe my pains and difficulties are going to be eased up humongous. My son did not want me to have surgery. I understand that may have been the father's worry, too. I write as if I'm not going to make it; the truth is, you never truly know. It's just minor surgery and hernia repairs, but my mind is on the fact that you never know what happens in the theatre room. So pray, be brave, believe all shall be fine, and have hope as you already started the day being thankful to be here and you here to repair.

The second week into the job, oh, I say, it feels as though the journey is getting quicker. I guess that because I generally use the time when I'm sitting to kind of not think too much but just write accordingly what I feel and have digested throughout the day. It was a strange day, one of those days when you were kinda touchy-feely at the beginning with all emotions. It steadied pacing throughout, like I just couldn't wait to be home. The train looks full. Yes, there is space to get on, but I genuinely would rather wait for the next one. You have to be in the right space of mind to be able to stand the journey, and mine is quite mellow. The next one approached straight away, so it wasn't too long a wait.

Living in the city of London can be quite complex in emotion. You get the hustle and bustle of it always moving. Then, at times, you want to shut out from the hustle and bustle to be able to retreat to peacefulness and calmness. Something is always happening. It can be fun at times, but other times its novelty can wear off.

So, my journey home is no longer direct. I need to get there earlier and wait for someone else to get there. Such is life at times that in order to get to that destination, one must achieve that goal. A block will occur where there is no ultimatum but to submit and go with the only option available to change direction or from the same region, awaiting the latter to arrive at a different time to allow you to proceed with where you're attending. You could be trying to pass a test, trying to court a relationship, trying to get home, trying to get another job, or trying to get healthier. There are so many alternate route options available that, at times, the block doesn't occur so obviously early on to help redirect you, but yet you are aware when you take the time to look that there's been no change. It's not until you're forced to stop that you realise, damn, I actually ain't going anywhere. I need to pick myself up and get on.

So, how was this morning's journey? To be fair, for the last few weeks, my left knee has been hurting. I've believed that it has to do with the direction of life pulling me elsewhere, as it is my legs that move me forward; it only tends to occur when climbing upwards, and well, I usually read that Louise Hay book of *Heal Your Body*. So, I guess the affirmation is that I freely flow with the universe. Many opportunities lay ahead for me, and I wilfully walk to accept them with ease. I don't know that that is the case. That is just what comes to me.

I also, for so long, hadn't had friends. Well, I did, but when I prayed for clarity, it was more clear to see who loves me with their heart for me. My friends have been a godsend; they think I'm crazy in a good way and recently have been calling me inspirational. I have no idea what I do for them apart from being me and sharing my love. The journey seemed complex in knowing who my friend was because I had a wall-up of protection from getting hurt. Hurts in the past can sometimes cloud how you see others who try to enter your life. I believe I'm over that, somehow miraculously making it work in the nick of time. There was no way I would come in fifteen minutes earlier. Sometimes, you have to not be so hasty and be calm. I'm such an eager soul that I can't help but please others, but I want to please myself first. It is better to be stress-free at work than stressed now. So the journey has been pleasant, and I've just arrived. Peace be with you, and have a blessed day.

So, my day was quite complex. As soon as I got in, manager was like five minutes earlier. Please, if you can help it, I understand if there was traffic. I was like, OK.

Then I couldn't wear my hoody. There is no uniform for now but to wear black. I kind of felt drained today, unappreciated, and yeah. It was just one of those days. The best part of the day was to see smiles on people's faces until there weren't any. I think I may have done something stupid today. I hope it wasn't. But I slept on it. I was offered a full-time role elsewhere with more money and basically, like I mentioned, my dream job. However, when they offered it, they asked if the pay was OK. I said yes at first because I was overwhelmed with excitement. Then I thought about it and was like, well, if this is an offer, that must mean there must be a benchmark of which the salary must remain, say, if you're happy with the offer. I mean, I had not been in this position before, so I thought to myself, OK, my situation is going to change. I'm going to be solely dependent on this wage and financial assistance. I need this to cover my household medication, food, school lunches, gas, electricity, food for lunch at work, and ermh, transportation. Will it actually suffice? Alongside insurance and other outstanding stuff like student loans, they are beginning to go over that threshold. It can feel good to get a higher salary, but it needs to be more than enough to get by. Just enough sometimes still kinda leaves ya making means for more. So, my phone has been out of reception all day. I have been so anxious that I pray to God that I don't lose this opportunity because I am viewed as greedy. But I just thought it was actually courageous to be upfront, not beat around the bush, and straight up ask for what you want. I did not even demand the exact amount of a raise. I said at your own discretion, I must, you know, be compensated a little for not trusting to take me on first. I'm a workaholic who enjoys having my own schedule of work and allocating my time accordingly to fulfil the role. So yes, now is the waiting game. It has been full moon seasoning time right now, and my instincts told me to take the risk and ask. You don't know if you don't ask. It could be rejected, but hey, with the law of attraction, you have to at least be willing to take a few steps towards your own desired outcomes. So, that was my attempt at manifestation.

I can't believe I'm sitting here on the train at 7.20 p.m. on my way home. I should still be at work, but everyone left. I wasn't about to allow myself to be abandoned without possibly knowing what the hell to do. I am so shattered, so tired, so anxious about the potential response, and so scared at the same time because I want better for myself and my family. But me, with my big old mouth, at times, goodness me. I count on God to take this into his hands. This role is meant for me and shall be as desired. A contract will appear shortly for me with an adjusted payment. Say it, spray it, and believe that it is possible, but you really have to believe that it has been received already.

I have been watching this pastor on Facebook, and even he says now is the time for powering financial abundance and prosperity and rising and rising up in my life. I believe that the opportunities lay out themselves right away. I even discovered that I'm not the only one who feels a certain way. Some of the team noticed that even a cleaner gets paid more than a therapist. When you're a mother and working, it's really hard to deal with not being able to pick them up from school, be there for dinner, or tuck them up in bed. I say thank God for the weekend. I can catch up with them, spend time with them, and make more memories.

In life, we think we want something, but then when we get it, it's like, oh my God, that's not what I wanted; that's not how I expected it. Perception, expectation, illusion, and reality are all so different when time hits. Goodness, I do think I chat a whole load of kafuffle le at times, but I'm sorry if that bores you. Haven't you gone through difficult choices and worried? Today, I was straight to think, oh yeah, let's get on the property ladder and buy our house. But Mumma reigned me in a bit with my excitement and was like, It does not fit your needs it's too small. I appreciate her so much. I appreciate a lot of people in my life for their constant love and understanding of me. Is it due to my bipolar disorder that I come across as indecisive? I'm not sure. But today wasn't a good day at work.

It was really one of those non-thinking kinds of days. Not even a mind wanders literally in the space of time, going with the flow. Sitting on the tube home, I watch the passing passengers either reading a novel, writing on their phones as I am, hugging couples, or the singer holding her mic stand, journeying from or to a gig. The irony is that I have to notice the singer. It was a good day; I guess there was a slight glumness to it. It was Thursday, one more day until break to the weekend. There is a tendency to feel a bit worn out. This life is completely different from the alleged dream of perhaps cruising in the sunshine, sunbathing, shopping, drinking cocktails, and being carefree. I sure wouldn't mind being on a beach right now, walking through some sand. Who knows, maybe one day that will be the case, but even I could get bored of that, or would I? I mean no worries, no bills, perfect health, an overflowing bank account, and the luxury of time to enjoy with friends and family. Helping those in need in their free time. You never know what could happen one day. But right now, I long for my bed, a lovely hot shower, a gentle drink of Baileys, and then sweet dreams and cuddles from my babies and husband that sound perfect to me. Sometimes, you can be in the mood to cook, write, or do most things, but tonight is one of those nights where even writing surpasses me. I will take a breather and return to you later. Have a lovely evening. Chillax, relax and unwind while you can.

Starting on the journey to work, it's Wednesday. We've made it midweek, wahoo. It sure feels quicker and quicker each week when you just get on with the day, regardless of what may happen. I feel kinda chirpy and keep talking to strangers as if I guess I've known them all my life, but they've been responding back. A lady nearby gave me a heart attack to start with as I was waiting for the school bus with my son. She saw my foxy fur jacket and just started rubbing me. I was like, argh, oh my God. She was like, good coat, good coat, seeing the warmth I'm in and feeling it from afar, strange. Then I go to wait at the stop lady, who is wrapped up head to toe, just the face not covered. I said to her looks, "It's like you're enjoying the snowy weather."

She was like, "I'm trying; I'm just gutted I'm not wearing a mask." She notices the difference when her face is covered. It was nice that we talked about all the strikes that are occurring in London, the trains, buses, nurses, etc., as the bus was running late. I said, "It's the travelling that knocks you out of working."

She was like, "Yeah, definitely." She appreciated the days she had to work from home as she had just recovered from a horrid cold. I said mine occurred in October and kinda felt like COVID. She said that she even tested to double-check that she didn't have it. I was like, "These scientists and doctors keep on coming up with new names for all these colds. For now, it's strep A. I think they are having too much fun experimenting." We laughed and were cordial. So, three of us were waiting, nipping and shivering in the cold. I say three is a magic number, and so is one, the unique one. I think I'm going to get to work when I can. For now, I'm still running early, and then the 251 appears to be packed on the bus. I prayed, saying, "Please let me on; I want to arrive on time." Then one comes, and it allows me to come on. It's amazing the magic of one, yet it was only me of the three that needed that one. I was grateful for the blessing and knew this was going to be a good day. Well, it better be. I feel it in my fingers that it will be. I wonder what news I will receive. How will the day at work be? I still have a stock take to complete, even though I can't really make sense of my notes, but I guess that means I'll have to redo it. That doesn't seem to bother me. I prefer keeping busy with myself or directly helping a person or group, be it a treatment.

One of the strange things that did occur for me today was that I was awoken from my sleep as my dream tended to finish at one thirty a.m., and I went to bed at nine forty-five p.m. My body felt like that was enough sleep. I checked WhatsApp to see if there were any messages and noticed my friend had messaged in, so I needed to share that with the guests for my party. Then I got a response saying, "Why ain't it free? I felt like she was a psychic offering to do readings." It takes a lot of energy. But nonetheless, she was up. I thought I needed tea. I eventually got myself up and was productive, made my packed lunch for the day, and returned to sleep at three a.m. See three is showing up in my day this morning. I'm quite into numerology and the patterns of life. I went to sleep and was awoken by my intruder alarm at six thirty a.m. I was like, "Oh my God, what's that?" Then I realised it was the alarm for if someone had broken in. I was lost as to what to do. It was just me and my two boys, thankful that they had slept in my room. I got straight protection from them. I looked outside the window to see if I could notice footsteps of someone breaking in from the back. Then, I was still feeling a hesitant worry, like there couldn't be an intruder. Then I tried to reach for my phone to see if I could call my husband or check the camera on my phone to see if there were any intruders, but I just sent him a text. I got up, getting ready to deal with this intruder face-to-face, and then I saw the light on downstairs. *Now, what intruder would switch the light on to see clearly? They keep the light on to distract you from seeing the face,* I think. But then something inside me said to call out Daniel. "Daniel, is that you?"

He said, "Yeah."

I was like, "Amen, hallelujah, praise God because I was so not ready to be tackling again to get out of my house." It's usually best to let them leave with whatever it is they came to do thief than face them on the cautious side of me. He said that the alarm hadn't sounded when he came in, so he thought it wasn't on. But hey, all is safe and sound and up for the day. But me being me, I think there is much more to the sound alarming than it is just alarming. It's a sign to be ready for this day. It is a sign of being attentive to my surroundings. This morning, my surroundings have been pleasantly welcoming. But sometimes, people's welcomeness can also be the perfect disguise. There is an underlying agenda that one may be unaware of, so be alert and be aware. There is much to do today, even if I'm unsure of what to do for the day. I already logged in and have trust issues, but I believe I have a diplomatic, positive approach to life. So yeah, like I said earlier, come what may. But this is not my last day. Well, it sure better not be. I know each day is really not a guarantee or promise. So I'm really grateful to be present in it. The words abide with me come to mind, so I abide with the day and, ermh, you know, walk with the Lord because we're never alone, now are we? Or are we? Or are you? Next stations mine Adios amigos.

On route to work, I sit down in the tube as it's so packed this early morning amongst all these service alterations. I tell you, it's all good once you're there at work, but it's just another story of pulling yourself out of bed to get there at times. I mean, I have been doing overtime on my body as a whole, training hard in the gym, then a full day at work, and don't forget the commute. I did not realise how much pressure all those activities were having on me. True, say you have to allow time and space to recover, or you just pass out. That has been me passing out. Finish the work train at the station and walk home. I go home, have dinner, shower, play with my babies, then sleep. That's what it has been this week. The early gym sessions have caught up to me. It's like trying to rebirth your physical self, and to be fair, what are some of the things a newborn baby does when born? Sleep, sleep, sleep, so this new body that was trying to break through also needs sleep. Talking about sleep makes me want to have sleep, but I can't do that on route to work. I have to wake up wake up. I can't believe I nearly completed my first full month here already. It is what keeps ya attending. We all want that pay day at the end of a month of hard work. God knows how much I'm finding out too.

New Starts

First day in a new job role——oh, how nerve-wracking of a day to start! The curiosity of worrying about how your team will respond to you. What will they say? How will you get on? Are they supportive? It was a great first day, I think. Maybe I'm too kind of a supervisor, but I think it's always a great leadership way for the team to find you approachable as a friend to be able to come forth with the issues they are facing and ideas of what they think could improve it. From what I gathered today, management listens but just listens, and deals with things in her own way. Not particularly in a way that the team understands. But as a supervisor, I can see the manager has been looking at the picture as a whole; hence, a whole new team from scratch and new systems equals new processes. It puts you in a position where you can't avoid it, but make sure you work as a team to overcome obstacles and support one another. I noticed the board had stars, which weren't being used. I look around and can see things that I want to change and improve.

But at first, I still had to remain focused on my own self-improvement. New starts don't just occur in one place. When they start, they occur in every single aspect of your life. It's a complete transition. My husband and I both had new starts at the same time, in the same week, just on different days. Mine was kinda a head start, as it began before him, but even though they were days apart, they felt like milliseconds apart from each other. Having two sons with autism and bipolar, my new start was quite a transition. We both entered into full-time positions. Mine be it the day, his be it the night. The first few days were like a shock to the system for both of us. Our roles at home just reversed immensely right before my eyes in real-time. It was quite crazy.

Now I'm not the typical housewife at all, and I haven't been in a while, not because I didn't want to but because I had the capability to not need to be. My slack in those duties meant I had time to focus on what was going on with me, finding myself getting myself back to me. While my hubby supported my slack and had my back with everything, he really is my better half. I'm the type of person who views his presence at home as working from home to be well. I'll step back and allow you the time to be with your children.

I went back again, and guess what? It was my first day at a new job once again. But this time, a new job starts within the first week of the new year. I thought, *I was nervous about the last one that I started, but nope, the nerves I had starting this one were way beyond that. I think it is because I hadn't actually stepped foot in the building where I was based. You know what? I'm so freaking proud of myself. I did it the first day, and I already want to do some further research so I can be the best I can be in the job role.* I'm now a senior complementary therapist in oncology. This is big for me. It's big in its purpose of helping to alleviate the pain of those with cancer through the administration of reflexology and aromatherapy. Who would have thought I'd be here ten years later from training? I feel so honoured to have such a role. It is going to make a difference to those who are fighting, and being part of a healthcare team that aims and strives to do their best for patients is an honour. I spent many days myself as a patient, and I feel grateful to be back on the carer side. I think nerves are a good thing. At times, we can fall into the trap of underestimating ourselves. It's not as easy to blow yourself up. But we need to realise our worth and the importance our purpose holds in life. I am a kind, loving, caring, and devoted person in my circles. At times, some have led me to feel that I wasn't because I chose to break free from them. So I could walk my journey alone, without distraction or gossip. Tending to other people's needs, especially with a terminal illness, means I need to be clear of mind and clear of negativity. I guess it is my view of how I try to be pure in thought and intention by having my whole surroundings cleansed. The new year was the ultimate time to cleanse everything. As much as I have returned to smoking again, I'm sure I will nip that bad habit in the bud. I think I do it for the sake of it. Not because I need to.

So, what did I enjoy on my first day? I enjoyed the new timing of waking up and preparing dinner the night before. The journey to get there is long, as there are a multitude of routes to get to work should there be any strikes. There were some strikes today, but nothing that caused great disruption, thank God. I enjoyed the peacefulness of my surroundings. The friendliness of staff. The aura within the working environment. And generally, just the slight change in how my nerves calmed. I met my manager and colleagues, and everyone was so friendly. Isn't it so blissful when work doesn't feel stressful, and there is clarity of organisation amongst the whole? It's only the first day. I know I will experience many things here, but for now, let me rest my mind. Be grateful I made it through the day, and my doubts were only silly worries that did not serve me well. If you're having a first day today, how is your first day going? What have you noticed? Give yourself a pat on the back that you made it, and be grateful that you're in the present moment. It's all we got.

Feelings

I tell ya, these emotions and feelings sure have a kind place of their own. They spring up on me so randomly, fueling me with feelings that don't make sense. I'm angry. That is what I sense—filled with rage and heartburn deep inside. But from what? I even have no idea where this is stemming from or why I'm getting so low. Most times, I believe these feelings are not my own but just someone transferring emotions onto me as a means to connect with or reach out to me. The moment I pick up the phone to arrange for medication to help stabilise these moods, it is like something wants me to start being OK, or the heaviness lightens on the moods and moves to my physical body with aches and pains.

I feel like I'm dying within myself. The mind thinks it wants to be frantic, scared of being present; souls are just searching, lurking around. It's like I'm slipping into another time zone. I feel like I'm useless and being so hard on myself. I am deeply disturbed and anxious within, of which I have no idea. How can I be happy and free when something unhinging is disturbing me deep within?

Changes are always occurring constantly in our lives.

Does your excitement get the best of you? Yes, it does indeed. I'm the type of person who gets so excited when excitedly happy about an occurrence. I literally feel like I can't control myself in the sense that I want to explode with energy because the excitement has sent all this adrenaline in. In the most positive. It's like when I laugh, or, you know, really laugh, because something is overly hilarious, I almost can't talk and could also choke from the hysteria of amazement at the humour. The danger of joy is so great that your body's ecstatic and laughing at itself in shock of its own reaction to laughing at a joke or situation that the body can't handle, even if it's too funny. Issues or not, lmao.

Don't ever allow silence or response to a question or answer. Dictate a negative feeling within you. It does one no good. Because the negative feeling makes you feel anxious and worried about the what-ifs and the what-nots. They are purely high-energy-sucking fields, which you do not need to have. After all, that is why I say sometimes it is nothing that is everything. That space of time can show you a lot. It shows you where you come up on the priority list of people to get back to. It also shows you simply nothing if you divert your focus elsewhere that where your attention is. It's no point in pondering possibilities that you can't control, especially if you're waiting for an answer. Focus on what you can do in front of you or what you have available to yourself. I'm sure there are many things that need doing. Like responding back to a meeting you're to attend, an appointment to go to, shopping, household chores, sleep, or cooking. How else do you occupy your time?

It was quite easy to keep falling into limbo, especially if one is used to multitasking. You can almost realise how much time you really don't have, especially during the winter when the shorter days sure do feel like that. Learn not to spread yourself so thin. But if you're spreading yourself, learn to delegate your time accordingly in a productive way. There is always a way when there is a will. Some things will take more time than others, and that is OK. So long as you remember that you are human, there is only so much your body can endure of multitasking, even if you're really good at it. Rest starts to feel like a luxury when you don't have it as a priority. Prioritise the importance of the very activities that allow you to be able to sustain the energy that you have to fulfil them.

I really have no idea what occurred this week. Towards the end, feeling demotivated, miserable, and serious. I blame it on the full moon. The full moon always tends to stir in new emotions, which frustrate and take up way too much energy. I much prefer the hyperactivity and excited moods, to be fair, as I feel more energised. But to be fair, my circle of friends around me appeared to be more hyper and energetic than usual; maybe I transferred that part of me over. Because their happiness did kind of keep me up-to-date and progressive about the days ahead. My dearest mate told me to keep thinking positively as all week I've been anxious about a job, even though I have one, but the new potential one awaits. I said, "What if they just cancelled my contract?"

She told me, "No" and corrected me straight away for thinking that way. She said to just leave it for now. You hear back when the time is right. I definitely appreciated that because I've even been trying to convince myself that silence can be a positive thing at times and that they are doing hard work behind the scenes, which does not really require you to be in constant communication about what is happening.

But I have such a curious nature. Yes, it was curiosity that killed the cat. I can't stand not knowing. I think that is why I also don't like surprises as much as I love them. Because I sense something going well in the past, when I catch on that something is going on, I'll see it as if someone is being deceitful and lying to me. Withholding information can be viewed as lying to me as much as it can be for your own good at times. Not only that, but it overwhelms me with great things. I don't want anyone to see my ugly cries of joy. Last year, my husband nearly gave me a heart attack. He surprised me on my birthday with my first-ever gold CD for reaching over 100,000 streams of my song. I was literally like, "No way; how dare you hide such a surprise so well from me that I had no suspicions?" I would just curse at myself, thinking no one cared for my birthday. It was just another day. I'll get the usual excuses. Oh, sorry, it's Christmas; it's not much. I mean, someone not much is usually something so much to me just for the sheer fact that they have even thought of me. Every effort counts, even if it wasn't much to them. Whenever asked what to get, I genuinely feel like I already have the gift of their presence in my life, which I'm truly grateful for. So I guess I make it difficult to get me because I'm not too fussy. It is really not about gifts but about the love that one gives. You can't put a price on that. December is the season to be jolly, *ta la la la la la la la la*.

I've been writing consistently for the last few weeks now. Some days, I have the flow; other days, I feel disappointed in myself as to what I'm doing. This is the point that I'm trying to get through with this book. The truth is, I'm just letting it be known that we are all humans, working through things in life as our own selves. We are all gifted in ways that even we can't see ourselves at times. It is normal to feel and think the way that we do. There is no specific book that really explains why your thoughts should be this way or that way. It is good to embrace yourself, so feel proud of your skin. I guess that is my point. I want you to remember how unique and fantastic you truly are and to maybe try not to be so hard on yourself. I know I'm hard on myself with my own expectations of myself, but I'm learning and trying to be better each day. So take each day as it comes.

Day ending of work can't help but feel like someone is really watching me upstairs. I had completed a seven-day work week. I was knackered. My shift ended with me being a massage model for three hours and a half, finished with a scrub and a lovely shower. Mind you, when I get home, the first thing I do is jump in the shower to wash my day off. I also heard some news from the new job, but they didn't give me much detail apart from saying they would call me about my salary. God knows I must think positively to attract positive news because the silence sure knocked me for the count, and the lady was just so busy. This is the issue when you busy yourself with so many things. I have a cake to hunt down tomorrow, a client to see, and balloons. Because some smart ass, yeah, I decided it is great to throw a birthday party a week before Christmas because it's my birthday. Vibes has been feeling differently lately, for sure. I got to celebrate as, who knows, Christmas is likely going to be quiet. I wonder when or shall I hand in my notice? I still have to be extra sure of myself and wait till I see that offer in writing. Hopefully, it will arrive soon. I can't believe I missed out on the holidays for work when I could be with my kids. Anyone that could all change. In my mind, I feel like my desires are being met but delivered in unexpected ways that are perfect for my own understanding. It feels so good to be coming home that bit earlier today. I sure hope dinner is done. My husband loves to hear my complaining from the moment the door opens to me.

So it seems like I feel sick in my gut; the unknowingness really messes me up. I'm ready to end one journey to start another, and yet I'm still in the waiting game for what on earth is going on. Midway through the moment of waiting, it makes me feel like, *what if that is what it is going to be like?* There are pros and cons to being part of a large company, but it is also not the same from the public sector to the private sector. Is the red tape all the same? How will they receive my calls regularly when I am unavailable to make calls? I don't know. But it was really bugging me a lot. I am a person who likes answers and knows where they stand. I think I fell apart; I do not know my own doing. I was so nervous upon meeting them virtually that when I got to physically come in touch with one of their centres, I was overwhelmed with joy, as it just felt kosher.

I feel naive, I feel stupid, and I feel vulnerable as I sit on the tube thinking over the plans for organising my birthday. A mate had told me why I don't let them do some psychic readings for the party and earn something from it. I thought at the thought of it as if, yes, that would be great at first. Then I reflect back on how interactions and planning to meet each other had been so impossible the last month. I kinda of felt like I had just been used. Is she only coming because she can earn from it, or is it generally to help me celebrate my birthday? I even asked when she was going to actually spend any time at my party, and she laughed. One would think I think too much about things. But I like that I sometimes want to please everyone and then put myself last. I genuinely have missed her as a mate, but the occurrences to meet up have often left me often confused and messed about. Why do we tolerate or put ourselves in situations that displease us? Or make us feel a way. Is it that something deeper is saying, "Let it pass, it will be OK, don't worry about it? Is it something reaching saying, they were going through something? This is only temporary." I don't know why it makes me sad. I get too excited about things, and then the big letdown gets me like a hard slap in the face. Am I wrong to feel this way? I mean, feelings are feelings. We all have them. But for some reason, just leaving work and having tried to make a phone call have brought about all the negative feelings that I need not have right now. It makes me tired to feel this way. I think I was also saddened by the man on the tube begging for money. He was on the tube yesterday, asking for food or money. I gave him all three sandwiches I hadn't eaten so he could eat. He couldn't even say thank you for that. Then I saw him again today on the Piccadilly line. I'm not sure if he was really homeless or not out of choice or forced, but I kinda sensed maybe he was not truly suffering as much as he was making out. He didn't look dirty. He didn't look tired, was very youthful, full of life with good talk, and was decently clothed, I guess. I mean, they do say it is illegal to beg on the tube. I need to pay better attention to those signs. The afternoon flock of people on the tube had a different flair about them. Some looked so lost, some were tired—I think a lot more tired—and some were just indifferent about the day. The majority of us are all in dark clothing where are the bright colours in the winter to keep our spirits up, eh? Maybe my feelings are once again not my own with the tube being so crowded and its natural depressive feel of suffocation.

I don't know why, but self-doubt tends to always creep in, as does the obvious overthinking. I can't harness it. I wish I could apply a better method, so I find writing helps in a sense to make sense of things. Maybe I need to get some meditation involved in my routine to ensure that I can best manage my emotions. As I've gone into the New Year, I've made a wide range of changes, be it in friendships, careers, personal life goals, or health. It is just like an addiction to want to do better. I think because my previous year started in a very different way with the second month of hospitalisation, I kinda worry and fear that it could happen again, but I will feel at ease, I believe, once I see my physical passing, a whole of having been in there. It's strange how we commemorate the traumatic events that occurred in our lives. Not to say everyone is the same, but for me, I've noticed that. I want that to change because, technically, our past does not define who we are today but shapes the person we become. I'm not in the stressful place that I was a year ago; I'm not looking after myself. I was more careful than ever before because the fall felt so hard at that time, and the recovery was nothing like I ever expected, so onwards and upwards. One must consider some meditation, which I have booked myself in for this weekend. Well, Pilates is similar to yoga a bit.

So I felt myself. Feeling confident and strong. Feelings of opportunities were lining up. How do I approach them? But the truth is to go with the flow and just get going with it. What you're supposed to do will come to you, leading you to the next door. So, as I try to grow and develop, I obviously have to take the first steps to activate what it is that I need to attract. I've started a new handbag collection, and I'm and going to start with my lip gloss. In order for it to grow, I must have a strategy. So, I approached a private club for entrepreneurs. I mean, social capital is vital to who you have access to within your environment and circle. So, I think I am going to chase up that lead and meet them. I joined one private club, but it just seems more like going out to nice places than building your network, so I think I'm going to cancel that one as it does not line up with the ultimate goal. I went onto LinkedIn to try to find some bloggers, publishers, and editors, so I have options to get my work out there. I've been approached by another company to get my music on their TV; trust me, there is always a small fee. Not everything that is free is always worthwhile it takes income to generate results. Or your time and effort in doing the work that you can for yourself. It's what they say: two minds can be greater than one. The more people you can connect with and share your missions and goals with, the more people tend to be interested in what you have to offer. You can't expand with people not knowing who you are. You really have to motivate yourself and get out of your comfort zone. When you are trying to level up and get to the stage and want that success, it's like a hunger rush. It's a process of strengthening your mind, body, and soul. It's a full workout, and you have to be on the ball. Success doesn't come so easily if you're not willing to put in the work. The key work tends to be on yourself before anything else can flourish from you. I feel like I am becoming a warrior, a fighter, and an athlete in training mode, trying to get to the end of line, as if I am back as a cross-country runner. Trying to get over the bumps in the ground.

So fricking happy and buzzing this morning, feeling good things on their way. New hair, new clothing—I just missed out on getting my next lip gloss line. The fact that I do not have any lipstick in the house drives me bonkers. Goodness, so I had a little talk with Mother Dearest. I can't help but share my excitement when I feel the possibilities of my dreams forming. Well, they always are. At times, it is when you reconnect with them that it hypes you up. And I get my mother excited at the same time, as I guess she is my best friend and partner in crime, not that I believe in crime. I do rant a lot about silly things. But it feels good to have joy. My name means it all the time, and yet it is ridiculous how, at times, I can let situations upset me so much. So the new positive—well, let's say a renewed positive mindset—is helping raise my energy. You know what's so good about that? Not having any drama attached? it's peaceful. Sometimes friends drop like flies from you so you can rise quicker without any baggage. I mean, if I need to get to a destination to save myself, there ain't no time to pick up things, but be ready and be prepared. That is why, I guess, there is also a chapter on training because life is lifelong learning. You're always moving forward when you try. There is no point in being stagnant, which means you can't go anywhere. But laying foundations takes time, and that time is spent understanding who the heck you are. Life sometimes makes us lose ourselves and forget what we are even about. No one wants to be waiting around in no man's land. There is nothing, but hey, I guess everyone is different, and not necessarily everyone aspires for things. Because, at times, nothing is everything. In a sense, I can say my nothingness gave me time to process and elevate. I'm sitting on the train and catch some bitch trying to cut their eye at me because I'm feeling myself. Dressed up in a bright green fake fur checked jacket, my own handbag design, Letitia Antoinette, and a turbin. It's like, bitch, please watch yourself. I am doing me. I know I speak my mind whilst I write. I got to the only way I know to be real. I mean, God told me gwan wrote another book and, like you know, present yourself and write because you have done know the first one was rushed because of your fast as being too bright. I mean, we are all chattering in our own minds, wondering, pondering whether we should do this. Should I do that? Oh, what if I did this? It's like, God damn it, stop thinking so much, and like Nike says, just do it, do it, do it, do it, do it. That extra do-it is so save the last dance, though. So yeah, it is good to also understand how your ego is, but you know, don't let it control you. You control it. Aite. These days are sure to pass faster when you feel good about yourself. The energy surge of greatness is spreading like a fire. My baby boy Casanova was like, Mummy, I love you this morning, and it just made my day. All around me are blessings. I feel healthy, and my babies and hubby are healthy. And as a family, we all have our own shared goals. To live the best life of happiness and joy. It comes in all forms, and at times, you know, we are blind to what we really have. So, appreciate what you have in front of you. Love yourself, treat yourself, and give yourself the tender loving care that you need. Don't rely on others to give you that, or you end up on no man's land. You don't want to go there. I mean, you learn there for sure because it is quiet, and no man's land for me is, I guess, your own darkness of trepidation that you got to get through the tunnel and trust that the light does shine eventually. But it starts from within you.

It has been a while since I've been here in feelings, but I have returned because all the random thoughts are exactly what they are: feelings of how I've been feeling through certain situations, and you know what? Sometimes, they're just randomised situations that I've invented for what they mean to me, when in theory, the reality is that no one is actually doing anything apart from keeping their distance. But in that, it feels like something;

the only way to remove that type of thought and way of feeling is to adjust the mindset to be more positive. Stop viewing yourself as a victim. If something doesn't agree with you, it is fine. Breathe in and let it go. Don't give it time to harvest you into something when there is no need of it. There is nothing wrong with keeping yourself to yourself, especially if that is what it takes to make one feel safe and protected within their own world. Don't guilt-trip yourself into believing that you must be engaging with everyone if it is not necessary. Everyone is meant for something in their own way of what's suited to them. It is OK to have compassion, but understand the boundaries of not making other people's problems yours.

Epiphanies

Little did she know that her life was about to change as she put out her cigarette and entered Camden Station. The day was quite straightforward, calm, and not too busy, but I still saw an old colleague who cancelled their treatment upon seeing she was the therapist. Each day over the last two weeks, the last treatments happened to be Sagittarians. Stressed from head to toe in the body. With similar problems, it is difficult to realise how one feels to those who care, but it is easier to do so to a stranger they may never see again. But why? She asked herself. What was so peculiar about this moment that such a transition lay ahead? She questioned herself, as she always does. Talking to herself while talking to whoever is holding this page. A part of her is receiving an epiphany, a download of information that floods the gates of the horizon. It blocks the present self from seeing, recognising, and acknowledging exactly what is happening; it is always this way for her because she gets too excited when new things are happening and keeps letting things slip and pass her by. Well, these times have come to a halt now. She must tread carefully if she wants to proceed to the next steps. The next stop is Kings Cross St. Pancras. She gets on to change lines Piccadilly as she gets on. She hears a man singing while wearing his air pods effortlessly. Should she get the middle escalators or the right up, she takes the middle, and the singing man continues up the right. Next, tube platform six arrives. She sees it is hers, but it is too busy one minute for the next stands to walk into an empty carriage.

How exactly is her life about to change? Is she going to bump into someone, meet a stranger, and find a sign on the tube? God knows not her. She just went with the flow of the route to arrive home as she finished work. But the feeling that something is happening in the background that she is unaware of is lurking loud and clear. It looks like she saw a sign and tried to log in to Facebook while underground. We said something was happening in the background, yet not sure what. Then, to her, the answer was backstage, a site to apply for acting jobs, where lead characters pay $60000 for twelve days of work. Suppose you can visualise if you apply; what would be the reason why not? She questions herself. Is it about the money, is it about the position, is it about the opportunity, or is it about set goals and dreams that one longs to achieve? Many have always said she should be an actress because of the way she changes her looks so many times. Yet she is forever on her phone, trying to write stories as she feels she is in her own movie, watching herself day to day. Thankfully, today she ain't in bed, just bingeing on Netflix, loathing, and feeling sad about the world. She knows there is a light that is glowing brightly; it has ignited within. She knows her husband is doing his best for them to be in the film industry. But this lady, who likes to be known as the Duchess is a strong, independent, awoken woman who just has not been so in tune with herself lately that she plays games and taunts her own ability to succeed. Today, the pastor said that all your heart desires will manifest. She didn't dare lock into that season because when it starts happening, she gets scared shit out of how on point God is. What do you know about God, eh? She is always lost in conspiracy theories about how things occur. But deep down in her hearts of hearts, she believes God is each and every one of us. It is just that some people you clearer than others. But doesn't it say in the bible fear not man but God? So if that is the belief, then one must fear everyone, but, oh my goodness, they must not be men. How would one know for sure of the existence of other species?

Many write in films of all these different species that exist with powers, etc.

What if they exist? How would one truly know? How do we really occupy time? Hmm, this could be the problem with the duchess. When she thinks too much, she wanders off into different realms. After all, she is a Rahanni healer. They may work within the fifth dimension, but she knows the teachings show so much more than that. What vibration and how fast are you truly travelling? Is your soul aligned with your present self?

Near Deaths

Have you any idea what it feels like to wake up physically from a death? Many years ago, hearing something like that, you think that was crazy, but in the times we live, it's like you just can't be surprised.

I remember how my first experience was. I felt like I had gone back in time to the time when I felt like I was being kidnapped. By now, I am not sure what they are called. They looked like Sumauris, but they were from Egyptian Arabic, and with the head covered, the scarf almost ninja-like, I think, but they camouflaged the tips of their head scarves to the curtain parts when they went up with that curvature. So that time was an awakening, and I was in the onyx ward. The point in tryna get to this time, 2022, was when I woke up from Asif feeling the wounds of samurai swords, and the trick to avoid death was to not be present in terms of mind, body, and soul. Like, huh, so at one time, the body of someone may have experienced such a death through healing. I've connected with the deaths and losses of many others with hypersensitivity. It runs through my body as unexplained pains and sensations, but to be alert to the vibration says it all.

Rejections

Follow your instincts the very first time around, and don't hesitate or question what you feel or what is true. Keep control of your time and order of alignment. If you hesitate, it could cost you your destiny through pure disbelief.

I sit on the hammock alone, thinking and contemplating whether I am loved and worthy. How am I going to get through this day? With joy, love, and hope, I have the strength to live on.

Lord, I am thankful for this day.

Thank you for my life. Thank you for everything you have blessed me with.

Thank you for my family, for my health, for my husband and kids, and for my skills and talents.

Thank you for the opportunities that are coming my way.

But I ask you, Lord, can I have some clarity on which is the best for me?

All you can do
Is love yourself well
Pray to the Lord that those prayers get answered.
Supposed to do better

Not be disappointed in oneself.

I am so happy when I hear good tidings from others.

It's time for good tidings to come my way. I'll be patient, as I need time to clear myself.

My babies are growing, and I keep missing out.

The industry of music entertainment just business demands lots of attention.

Attention, I would rather be focusing on my family. I love them, I do, and I miss them so much.

But I am sure that they have grown to not need to worry about Mumma too much.

I entrust my life to y'all.

I've tried, and I psychologically messed up or metaphysically, as my beliefs seem much too strange.

Childhood ain't the same new generation's lane. Children are our future. The greatest gift of all is to create and birth a child. I wonder—I wonder what life would be without me. I see it, and I feel it seems lonely—no time to pity oneself, get revive oneself, get alive, and be true, not blue.

I've always longed for the best. I always get the best, but I am, we are, they are, he is, she is, but altogether, we are one.

Appreciate all that you have given and been blessed with, for days are gifts and blessings that should be celebrated.

When I reflect on the way certain situations make me feel or the way that I respond, it is clear that I have been partially scarred by some experiences. One of the key ones that tends to hinder me is the feeling of fear that I'll be incapable of fulfilling my roles. I fear that I am going to become so hyper-manic that I'll need to be sectioned. I just fear that I am not doing well enough and am going to get let go. Also, anxiety that everything was just going to come down crashing. The importance is to do your best not to think negatively, or it will just eat up and eat up at you to the point you just start losing yourself over nothing but the thoughts in your mind.

I am in such a good mood today, which feels great. I don't know why I question why I feel good, but I do. It is just my nature to question everything. I've been singing since morning. My voice is always changing; I've been dancing. Maybe I am getting excited about my birthday. It was great to get excited during this time thirty-three years ago. It was getting tighter and tighter to move around, being coached up in my mother's belly, kicking to get out, to see the big, wide world. So, four more days until birth day. Oh, I am a drama queen. I guess it comes with being a mother. Maybe I get just as excited about how I was feeling when it came to my son's being born. Do you ever try to remember what it felt like to be a baby? Guess most likely not. But I was good. I didn't cry. Of course, I cried, but I was quite content because Christmas just followed the exact week after, and I think I came earlier than what was expected. I'm not sure; I'll have to double-check. So yeah, what else came to me? I noticed as I changed the central line. Friends meeting along the way, it was so beautiful hearing the joy in their voices of just bumping into each other on route to work. It was like you could feel a sparkle. You could just notice it. I mean, I don't ever notice the joy in people's reactions to seeing me. Well, I do with some of my friends, just as it is for me to see them. But I kinda get overwhelmed or lost in the moment, as it is a shock to my system to see a friend and interact in my home with someone outside of my household who lives in my household. I just get taken aback by faces for some reason, but in a good way. I look at my reflection in the window, almost not recognising myself in my brown turbin and hoops. I felt I looked like a Nubian queen. I almost gave myself a heart attack. Oh my God, I am so extra. I mean, how often do you actually look at yourself on your journeys? I kinda of forgot what I even left the house in and just put on some clothes with no thought to it.

So it looks like I was right. It was going to be a good day. Come into work to find out I'll be finishing early because of my annual leave entitlement for two weeks in Wahoo. Truly, I didn't have a choice as to which days, but one can't complain they got to come back home early. There are a few things I need to do in preparation for my party, like get the fruit and vegetables, maybe some more drinks one cannot have enough for Christmas, and I definitely want to be merry merry merry. I even got a Santa coming that's going to be giving gifts out to everyone, which is kinda cool for me. I need to get a stocking filled with the gifts, I think. I can also return the empty helium can that was sold to me on their cheeks, eh, goodness me. I think I'm gna get my cooking on today. Those three extra hours of work gave me so much time to try to sort some things out myself. I am grateful.

So, I'm literally so shattered. This was my first full week, Monday to Friday, in my full-time job working within the role. The whole routine change of getting ready, getting the train, walking to work, and adjusting to new systems and processes. I didn't realise how overwhelming or shocking it can be on the body. I've literally wanted to go straight to bed from work most days. It takes a while for the body to adjust to change just as much as it does emotionally. I process information quite quickly, and I do pressure myself intensely without even realising it at times. Somehow, I learned a whole new system of recording patients' notes within the day with just one error, which shall be rectified on my return on Monday. I was grateful to treat patients today on the practical side, so that was nice. Now it is time to step into my role as mummy. I have the kids' homework to supervise and my son's most recent project to make his own shoes, which is amazing. We just need to support him to get the necessary tools so he can get started. There is no need to be so hard on yourself, but if that is the way you programmed yourself, so be it. I am just being mindful to rest, relax, and listen to my body. I've sent my son the necessary tools he will need, and now I've directed him to eBay to research the costs of the materials. I am so proud that he has found a passion for something he is interested in. So I've booked myself for Pilates tomorrow. This should be good for destressing my body. I shall make sure I take myself to the spa and unwind, as it's needed after a long week. Life really is amazing when you start believing in yourself and allow the old you to go and the new you to be born. This new me is reading more, exercising more, spending more time with my family, taking care of appearances not just for me but the whole family, exploring new businesses and ideas, and learning new skills in a new job. A new way of life has one feeling more hopeful about the future.

Lately, I've noticed I'm just not too quick to get excited about things or situations. It has very much gotten to the point where, it's to be, I'll patiently wait and see. But does the seeing actually come into formation? And if so, how does that feel? Life feels very strange for now; I think there is a part of me that has disassociated with a lot. To prevent disappointment. It is one of those ones where there has been a part of your life where you longed to be connected with groups or a circle of colleagues or friends that just appeared superficial. Then all I care about is my family's happiness, my children, and my husband. I want to do well at work so I can keep my job and provide for my family. There is some importance there to ensure a good rapport within that environment is established. I do like to be needed to help others, and I can do that. I don't think I lost as such, just noticing how quickly time flows. We are halfway through the third month of the year. I feel like I was stuck in January for years, which is strange. But what more can I say? I think it is a universal experience all around the world where people are not exactly sure what is going on in their lives. But they feel something is there without truly knowing what it is. I am praying for all the good things.

It has come to my attention that little or often, and I've tended to think it was OK to share my ambitions, goals, and dreams with others outside my household. But it has proven to be a negative move in how they perceive me. It often comes to my realisation that not everyone is for you, and not everyone is your people or tribe of like-minded people. It felt like a deflating word when I opened up about my aspirations of wanting to be a prime minister. I am the type of person who feels anything is actually achievable. I don't find many things to be bizarre, only bizarre when it seems that stories match the actions of what they claim they are doing. Or when you notice they actually have no idea what they are doing but the means of the capital to splash without the added discipline to see things through, spreading themselves thinly and caring so much about what social media has to say about it.

Being alive in these times feels so lonely with the damage of social media. Because I just feel like people are not people any more. Because many are so conditioned by the media, they limit the understanding that we are all unique and can achieve what we truly desire in life. So long as we move forward, don't give us the power to dishearten us. I've been thinking a lot about where I intend to be in the next few years. Before, I longed so much to pursue music, but when the opportunity arises, then comes the other attachment of allowing yourself to be controlled and told how to dress, how to do one's hair, and what songs to sing, but a payment is also an added bonus. That is why some things are make to outgrow and outlive themselves. Because by the time the opportunity comes, it is like, "Nah, that's not for me, I've learnt." I've seen a lot about this industry, and for me, it stinks, and I don't like the person I have to become to endure it. That is when you know it is time to move on when you have to force yourself to partake, and everything you do is seen as great, which comes so effortlessly to you. But then you think, would it really make any difference if it came earlier? Some things you do in your prime, some things you do because it is all you know how to do. So to save yourself from being in such a dilemma, it is always worth trying what you haven't done or the very things that bring you peace, stimulate you, and make you feel appreciated. You don't need to overthink it.

Another industry I had started up in with my entrepreneurial flare. Location and environment also matter for the success of many ventures. I am not for all this virtual reality of worlds, yet I think there is still time until that becomes a full comprehension of reality, as many movies like to show their predictions of this. The good old fashioned of seeing and visiting a store works differently depending on where in the world you're located; a website helps them find you in the neighbouring areas. Experience is still valued even to this day. Without it, then I guess what the point is? So, I noticed over the last few weeks that I was getting tagged in posts from my past brand ambassadors. I could not help but look over their joy to be a part of something I started, but also my efforts in creativity to promote them as their individual selves for the things they generally do in life, along with my gym wear. I literally had something going well for the everyday woman. Then, I guess the capacity of which I knew them disconnected, and I just didn't continue with that strategy, but it wasn't all failed because the tagging process showed to me a sense of belonging, which is great.

In my reflection, it is clear that ups and downs naturally occur in life. It is either how the wind blows, how the river flows, or how energy disperses where it needs to be. The importance lies in how you view and perceive yourself. I know in my own self I am quick to doubt my own abilities and capabilities, and it holds me back, but it is an everlasting process of understanding your own self. How and why we do the things we do. The response to life is everything. So, it is important to embrace the processes. What may have seemed negative at a time now may appear as it was, but with a disassociation of feeling towards it? Protecting yourself is key, and harnessing more positive energy helps to enable that protection. Quite often, as healers, we usually view ourselves within a protection golden bubble. I usually call upon archangel Michael for protection through God's love so that all angles and areas of my life are protected, and all negativity that tries to come at me is reflected straight back to the light. Should you ever experience harm from others, it does no good to send harm back but prayers and love. Let that be the multitude.

I spend so much time battling to try to be better, but my imperfections get the better of me. It takes time to grow, even within one's own self. I was contemplating today the realisation that my journey with the doctors has left a partial scar on myself. I feel a constant need to justify my actions and feelings as a means to get by. When in Heinz's sight, there is actually no need to. But it is a process I have learned from numerous times debating what medication works for me and what does not. In most cases, it didn't give me new symptoms. I have paranoia about feeling low, as with bipolar; too low a mood can be just as dangerous as too happy a mood. It is frustrating. Nonetheless, there has not been a discussion on ADHD, which was later diagnosed. So maybe that is why a lot of medications were hit-or miss because of other conditions. Who knows, but it sure is tiring going over in one mind over and over again the whys, ifs, and maybes of one's actions. I only long to be happy and fulfilled and have the energy to enjoy my family. But the negative emotions tire me out completely. This is exactly why I am trying to remain true to myself, so I need not worry about how others perceive or treat me. I am getting there. It was Friday night each day this week. It has been five a.m.: wake up, gym, steam, sauna, work, then sleep. I've been so drained that a part of my mind has delved deep elsewhere. It is almost as if a part of me is going into myself without realising it, and then there is the weather freezing cold and misery in spring. That pulls me down, but I'm proud that I am getting up each day and taking part in my life, not just sleeping it away. I am trying to get more time with my sons. I really want to support them with their studies. Heaven knows that if I was a bit more disciplined with my studies and most things earlier on that I attempted, I may be somewhere else. But that is not the way to think. In my eyes, that is too demeaning. Looking at the positives, I can encourage them to know what it feels like when they understand subjects and do well to maybe get them to want to do so on their own instead of computer games and YouTube.

Species

Some might think it strange to believe, but quite often, as the humans we are, we do question. What species is he or she from? Maybe because of the way one behaves or the things they say. But these are actual words of context that some of us use to describe a way of doing something when it is either new to us or feels completely out of this world. Is it crazy? I don't think so, lol. My thinking can feel so bizarre at times because I don't dare open my mouth to say these thoughts to just anyone. You know what I mean, lol. I would much rather put it in a book, thinking, *Meh, who knows who will ever read what I write?* I think I am all alone in this world, not even believing that I know what those things you are writing might actually reach the same catch of fish that you are from. You know your tribe of people. The ones that get your flow and your train of thought. *Strange? Right!*

Well, I guess when you kinda put it like that, it kinda makes sense to me. I mean, well, to say the least, just the other day, I mean, not just a day like I'm talking about a few years ago, right? Anyone who gets to the point, yeah, a few years ago? I was going through some experiences with my sight. Now you know we all have sight. Well, technically, not all, as some may be without eyesight. But for me, even without eyesight, we still get sight in how we see our sixth sense, our third eye, and our conscious self. I hope you are with me, as I will just be explaining things in the simplest ways of my understanding. So, I will try to break it down as much as I can so it makes sense.

So many years of walking, going to pick up my son, and kinda feeling on edge. Apart from me is feeling and seeing the world in a whole different light; right, we humans naturally say these things to I'm a whole different light. Now, technically, what on earth truly is a whole different light? How many different lights are there, really? Well, from the side of my eye, I thought, *what could I possibly think that flickered past my eye at this time of day? Then I thought, hmm, what did I just see flicker right in front of my eye? Just question myself and, like, oh, push it to the back of my mind.*

Now, in my mind's eye, I could have sworn I saw a bat fly by so fast, so quick, just like in Hotel Transylvania, I mean. It is not an impossible thing to appear or see; they do exist. But, hmm, in this day and age, you can't randomly say those things out loud to people. You can't even question or argue that what you think you saw is the term that would be used. Or that my friend will just be darn right: yeah, you got schizophrenia. Even without being under the influence of any type of medication, that is the thought that would go with a person who has been diagnosed with mental health, not merely a person who is more spiritually attuned.

I recall staring at the member of staff, and she avoided my eyes and then acting so suspiciously as if I were aware that I was seeing something that I potentially shouldn't be able to see with my raw eyes. You know, sometimes you get those silent senses that you both sense saw something but act as though it didn't happen amongst others, yet you stay humble as to I'm a keep quiet, not like anyone would believe anything I saw or admit that it is what you see. Because that is very much the way of the world, we see and experience many strange things, and when something is unusual or unexpected, it is not of this world. It is another planet, but yet this is Earth, and well, these birds and bats do exist.

So species, I believe that spiritually, our spirits do belong to different species.

How is it that some refer to themselves as lionesses, wolves, and butterflies? They are all species, which we categorise in this life all the time. As humans, we are categorised by blood type, skin tone, and the different places on earth where we originate from, even though we were born in a place here on earth. It is often noted that, apparently, we humans are also one of the most complicated species ever to live because of how complex and diverse the situations we get into in life are. I mean, we drive each other crazy bananas, and yet we love each other just as hard as we possibly can. Who would want to be without some? The common thing we say is that men are from mars and women are from Venus. I mean, who has ever been to Mars or Venus to know these things aren't true, and if that is the case, what exactly are the traits of a Martian and a Venutian? Hmm, maybe I should do some digging and research further into it, but nah, I am not going to go and do that. I would rather leave you with my unbacked theories and ponder your own opinions. I named this chapter species for a reason. Now, truly of the world, do you actually know how many species exist, and not just that, do mystical species exist too? I mean, we humans are forever fascinated by the TV of these random mystical scientific films, and where do these ideologies of such things come from? Do they randomly appear as visions in people's dreams and minds, and then they translate it to paper and put the visuals on it? I say, Yeah, pretty much sounds quite simple, like, wow, that's quite fascinating. *Ermh*, I guess so. Well, not really we're humans; after all, we have the same capabilities, right? So what is so unique about that? *Hmm*. I guess it depends on what you know, what you have been conditioned to know, or what you choose to educate yourself to know. I mean, some say we are all one, so we are all connected in some way or the other, right, but how?

Hmm, that's interesting. I guess we all have our own demons that we are facing, right? That is our saying; we say it right, like demons. That mental struggle of our own selves. If it is a mental struggle of our own selves, I guess we have to look really at who we really are. I can ask that question in the mirror: "Who are ya?"

Roles

We all play different roles in life. So many have many, so many have few and some might not think they play any roles in life. But in reality you being you is also a role in having to cater to yourself. The difference is that at times we almost forget how many roles we play in life. Not just that, but the time and devotion it takes to fulfil those.

In the workplace, you may just view a person in the role that they are assigned to do their job title because that is what is closest to the eye when within that environment, and so often, we can become blinded by the other constraints and roles they have to fulfil.

The typical role of a man may be seen as that of a boyfriend, father, fiancée, husband, brother, son, uncle, grandson, grandfather, godfather, great uncle, foster father, or sperm donor. The typical role of a woman may be seen as that of a mother, wife, girlfriend, fiancée, sister, aunt, grandmother, great-grandmother, godmother, sister-in-law, or egg donor. Yet some are without any of those roles. Not everyone who is born is a part of a family. In the first stage, some are abandoned and left until they become part of a family. And in some cases, as people get older, they emancipate from all such connections and are only themselves. Riding on the solo ride.

Nonetheless, the roles that we then enter into our lives vary, be it the career of our choosing. Or be it of the very environment that we are surrounded by. For some, all it is but war, a battlefield of pure destruction, and on the other flip of the coin, a nice bed, a home, and a routine job to get through each passing day. We all strive to survive through very demands that life throws at us.

How often have the roles that you have chosen to take up within your own life overlapped over another? Most of them tend to, I believe, and at times, those different roles are dispersed amongst each other in order of priority to get through each day. It is quite easy to lose ourselves in the different roles in our lives. We abuse some roles and can lose ourselves because we end up putting the very role of ourselves last. The importance of roles is vital in how you manage to get through each day because each of us, at our core, has needs and tendencies that need to be met in order to grow. When they are not met, I guess we meet with chaos, which can be fun at times but also destructive at the same time. It takes good balance and coordination to enable ourselves to be able to stand straight and right with our paths. Which roles in your life are important to you? Which roles are not so important to you? Which roles cause you great joy in your life? What roles cause you crises in your life? How shall you sustain your sanity while living your best life? Which roles enable you to do so?

Do you realise how important your role in your life is to others around you, or ever contemplate the effect your life has on another? We may come into this world alone, but we are supported and carried into that life to live a life of abundance, so how shall you fulfil your role and duty to yourself today?

I personally never realised or noticed that my role in my life had any effect at all on others. That was the naivety of my own soul. It is in paying more attention to myself that I recognise the difference that I make within my family unit, then also extends to the further extension of the rest of my family, friends and strangers. I recently have been sharing with the world my recent successes and struggles, but more so successes, and it's been abundantly consistently growing in a strange, beautiful continuum. I am truly grateful for what triggered the rejection from a publisher. They said it was not for them, but thank you and continue to write. I saw this as something I must continue to write, and the reason I was rejected was just as it was stated, they are not for me. Without any feeling of remorse, a gentle disappointment led to motivation to research more thoroughly and deeper within myself. I found publishers that are specifically seeking writers of mental health and underrepresented groups. Since then, my email has been receiving updates from potential publishers to submit to. I was then offered a new job position the following week. I was nervous and anxious before the interview because I thought I did not really know that much about them, but I do long to know more about them and develop my skills so that I am skilled for whatever ever next job role I go into. So, I gave it my all and also had questions prepared for them. In visualising how my journey could be with them in developing myself, I believe that led to the offer. I have not yet heard any further details this week from them, but as my conscious is aware that new information is due to follow, I shall wait patiently without pressure till that information arrives. Sometimes, that timing can give you insight into the schedule flow of work. To be fair, I do want it to be balanced because I have a full-time job. I was also offered to speak at a mental health and human rights conference for the month of July that same week. I reached out to them to find out. More details of exact locations, their other services, recommended hotels, etc. I told my friend about this, but something tells me that if I am to go, I guess I should use it when I am to go instead of that. I need to remember who I am as an individual. I shine brightly amongst people I don't know. Being in a room of people I don't know but like-minded people has always been a strong point for me. When I last shared a TV interview, they took my light off. Yes, tacticalness is vital. So maybe this is a journey you completely take upon yourself and follow through with. After all, solo artists generally share the stage to either gain more popularity, strengthen their position, or keep them relevant. My aim is to test my strength of light alone. But then again, there is no harm in being open and seeing how things go. So yeah, and the week after that. I passed my driving test. So, there is a flowing pattern of growth and success that I want to keep track of. My being me has been demonstrating to others my journey in how I reached that and now in how to sustain, maintain, and let that spread to others. But little did I know it was already spreading, and those around me are also feeling the great abundance of love, success, and joy being applied in such a miraculous way. They were not fighting it but acceptingly going with the flow.

So yes, we all have a duty to ourselves, and when you take that duty and role in full strength, that energy transpires all around to those whom you love. We are all connected. We have a role to fulfill. When you're true, you see life as fully renewed.

Manifestations

Oh, my fricking God. Do you know how overwhelming it is when good things keep happening? I mean, do you resonate with the disbelief that great things are happening? You get so happy that you could explode. Well, that's how I get it. I could actually punch myself into the realities that are occurring. Not just that, but in how fast it is occurring. It's like, Oh my giddy gosh, give me more. I can handle it, oh yeah. But then I actually feel like I am floating on cloud 9; you do know nine is a money number, though. I shall manifest for it to unfailingly continue to flow my way in all directions. The money call has come to me now.

I can't help but need abundance, wealth, and prosperity with great health in my life. I think it is time I do a check-up and a little MOT on my body. But next week is scheduled for nonstop training in massage, so I guess its arrival is already in the process of arrival. One of the greatest things I manifested was clarity. With the clarity of my realities, I began to see that everything was right in front of me, and a surge of purity filled within me to allow me to grasp it all with both hands. Some may think, what on earth are you on about? Like, really, yes, really, really, I wanted to turn my life around and get into a regular routine of work in an occupation that I qualified and trained for at the level that I suited for. I placed myself as a CEO quite a while ago so I could have that freedom to see what works for me.

As you know, I do divulge about a topic that I write about, as I just exquisitely get excited about the sheer realisation of it all. When things are going well in your life, I tell you it feels like you're dreaming, but that's literally the feeling of living the dream. We all have dreams and desires. Some may make out that, nah, I do not have any of that, but the sheer fact of being content is also a desire that is not always met.

So take a breather, relax, breathe in, and breathe out. What is it you desire? What is it you long for? Is it nothing, or is it something? I longed to be a superstar quite long ago, purely because I played a star in a nativity play when I was five. I even choreographed my own routine for the dance. While everyone else was an angel, I thought to myself, *Nah, I don't want to be an angel. That just does not pay enough attention for me and looks boring.* Oh goodness, if only I had a copy of the video to be able to recall that memory and see what I was like. You never know. Someone reading this may remember that I'll give a hint: it was at Tennyson Road primary school. I think it was the feeling of all the lights from the camera while on stage with the centre light on me while I danced my routine and the silence that I enjoyed from the audience that made it strange to remember those feelings from years on.

Sometimes, we don't realise that we ask for the things we truly long for in life from a very young age. So, as the superstar I longed to be from a young age, I couldn't quite reach that in person via the world, as you know. So I just began to keep visualising that, you know what, I am a star in my life. I shine brightly for my family and those who love me without realising it. You have to do the things you love. No one really knows me, but I know myself, and that is good enough. Besides, I always say God is my father, and damn, everyone knows God even if they don't believe. So what is meant for me always arrives in divine timing. I tell ya, divine timing can take seconds, minutes, hours, days, weeks, months, and years. Now that I am in that manifestation time of years of preparation to get to the point of, oh my God, I'm finally satisfied that it did help with praying for clarity in all my endeavours. I literally did wake up one day at literally start of this week with more clarity of sight to a lot of things. That felt like an internal understanding of the importance of the chronological timing of how things occur—as we say, all in due time, too.

I remember writing a five-minute book called *My Five Minutes to Fame*. It was a ten-page book that was rejected. I am like, oh my gosh. So I took the time to write more, and, well, I published myself. I would not use Grammarly again to do my checks, as it just does not work for me because of the way that I write. You must have noticed by now that I have a tendency to write as I speak, not in the best of comprehensiveness, but I try. You know, just bear with me as I am severely dyslexic, but have no fear: I am here to stay and connect with you and your vibe.

I still haven't told you the manifestations of my dreams that I achieved. I might miss out on the odd one or a few. I don't want to shock my mother. I learned to be my own best friend. I laugh with myself about the very thoughts and ideas that come to me. Most tend to think I am a little bonkers in a good way, OK? I became a singer-songwriter at the age of eleven. I was an athlete at a young age. I was the fastest in school. These things count: I was a sports coach; I became a life coach; I was a healer; I was a business mentor; I was a podcaster; I was and an author. I'm in the early stages; a mother, you think, comes first. I know, right goodness me, a wife. You know I am obviously someone's daughter. A post-production supervisor, a music director, a model, an actress, a beauty pageant queen, an influencer, the owner of a brand of gym wear, makeup, trainers, and jewellery, and a psychic. I thought to myself, like, what else? Oh yeah, a complementary therapist and spa supervisor, and you know what? I appreciate my hustle. You can manifest anything you long for in life when you try. By the way, yes, my music is online. Please feel free to check out artist Madame Kapuscinska. Thank you very much. And also a record label.

I may not be financially rich, but I am rich in ways that are unexplainable to me from my experiences and journeys in life. The way you value yourself and life matters. The way you view who you are and what you can achieve matters. Being a person who has been diagnosed with bipolar and ADHD, I often have to deal with the fear of doctors breathing down my neck about Letitia. I do prefer to be addressed as Duchess Letitia, but hospital records that I've been to don't allow that title on there, so yes, it's Mrs. I thought I'd mention that because I can. But in this book, I share with you my personality and parts of who I am.

Because I was lost in my own self, and I tell you, it is quite complex to find yourself again. Life throws many obstacles and challenges. The point of getting through them is to grow, learn, and discover yourself. The journey of the self is lifelong learning, no matter how old you are. I'm quite often told I'm an old soul. When I did some serious, serious meditation, I managed to find out that my soul age is eighty-four. I get along with all generations, as most of us do. But I think they then forget my true age when I come correct at a person for possibly crossing the line with me. Like I said, know who you are, stand firm, and know what your boundaries are.

Back to manifestations, I remember talking to an Uber driver who asked me the question. He asked what it was like to be an artist and live in London. I was like, it's cool people are kind. They leave me the fuck alone and allow me to be me. My fans come at me appropriately and let it be known that my music has saved them from feeling blessed. But having him say that, he was like, "What would you do if you were like filthy, filthy rich?" I was like thinking to myself. Who are you to think that I am not? I mean, I always said I'd have my own private driver. All these Uber drivers that pick me up tend to be in the latest Mercedes, which are such smooth BMWs. I do like the Kia's and many smooth-driving cars. I am materialistic in a different way than the efforts required. It costs about a bottle of wine in a restaurant or club to get to the other side of London. I guess it is secure. I am always on Lives, recording videos and singing on my journeys, so in a sense, my devices and the world generally know wherever I am. On top of that, my father's God guides everything. I like that I can afford my rent, my electric, my gas, my food, and my appliances in my house. I am forever in charity shops near my end, as somehow they always got new stock from pretty little things, and boohoo. The odd Louis Vuitton bag or Prada under £100. I really am not a tight person; I just value things differently. I guess I can be tight from time to time, but what I give out comes back to me in multitudes of multiples in miraculous ways from every angle possible, like a damn girl you just need to lift a finger. I even thought to myself, Gods is so awesome, yeah, he made it so possible for me to have the whole world's attention on me 24/7, earning an unfailing lifetime supply of abundance that just my living and breathing and being the amazing me keep the world functioning of the fascination of my mind. I had a mother-fecking episode one day that took me to the onyx ward. There were people in helicopters flying just to get a glimpse of me. I charged the whole damn world a twenty per cent tax seven years ago, if they ever use and realise what it is that I'm actually doing through my self-realisation through the laws of God's law and metaphysical law. I will shut your sh*t down. Every single place that I have lived within a twenty per cent radius of all those places will be blessed financially abundantly; every place in the world that I've crossed will have that, too. The people will just have to deal with themselves. Oh my God, I almost forgot to mention that I am also a pastor and doctor of metaphysics. Ask me how. I deemed myself qualified and bought the certificate. I got ordained just like that, Steve Tyler. Any who, I can't tell ya any more right now; it's like 3.54 a.m. I am an extraordinary individual, like everyone else. Trust me, I know people enjoy challenging me because they want to be billed by me. I have my own darn lawyer who is literally in the process of suing a whole university department. Imagine that it is occupational health. The irony is that a department is supposed to assist with the way of life. Don't watch that. I can't go into that story just yet. I got to go to sleep. I start work at eight thirty a.m.; it takes me an hour to get to work. I got to get washed, changed, and sort my own lunch. Ain't no man got to work too hard around me apart from understanding how to love and believe in himself. Many always tell my husband he is a very lucky man, but so many people said good luck,

Daniel, on our wedding day, and they really did. I mean, my whole family did. We St. Lucians are funny, delightful, and a joy. I mean, my name means to bring joy beyond praise. I've always said I'd come back to save my whole family, and people think that your family is like my family. If you saw who was at my wedding, even my husband never got to meet everyone. I had an open ceremony because, like we, God's children, we got permission from our family, as it is the Catholic traditional way in Poland, and the public congregation that attended mass on that Sunday was also able to be present for our wedding. That is what an open ceremony is. But God knows a person with a dirty mind, not like me, that all I was saying, hahaha, would think meant I had many husbands. To think of it, my husband's hand was shaking when he put the ring on me, and the priest splashed me on the face with holy water. I don't know, but I never thought that could have been a possibility until now, you know. Like, I mean Mormons, I think they the religion that got like thirteen wives or something some places in Africa also and also in the Asian culture, I don't know. But my husband is managing well for now. I tell you, God gives you all you desire—I mean desire. What do you desire? I also wrote a song called '*Got the Money, Got the Riches, and the Big Banks There*'. Oh yeah, I literally found a way to buy out all these banks and own them for myself. My first ever job was as a banker for Yorkshire Bank at the age of, I'll tell you, seven years old, Farley Junior. I cash up the money and everything and fill up the cheque. I just hand them the signage once I do all the leg work. Money flows to me effortlessly in magical ways. So, like, if I was a reader of this right now, I would be asking myself if this person is actually serious and actually explaining to me how she bills the country and the world for misconduct or something baloney in how she sustains her life.

She justifies her actions for everything she was blessed with. I mean, I know people say that some people think they are so entitled, but to be fair, she is a Duchess, legally a pastor and doctor of metaphysics. Hmm, I do not truly know if I can test her. I want her clarity. I need some clarity. No, this is wrong. I need money, money, money, money, money. How do I receive that? I mean, whoever came up with Earth universal credit, where does that idea stem from and not just that? Are you telling me that? I am so sorry for this duchess who speaks—I mean, does not speak, but writes. She was also a young consultant for this country, England, and the very health secretary that was in power was found to have her own island or investments in Harley's. I tell you no lies. They were called young advisors. She reviewed many of the papers in government from the top of this country and was paid only £8 an hour for her work. At fifteen, the other four would go into the business they had called yarn at the time. She later tried to open her own business called Young Advisors Foundation, but the bank just kept charging her business charges for her social enterprise, which put her into debt and led to further bad credit. Just as Yorkshire Bank also gave her bad credit at the age of seventeen when she was a minor, I mean, my, oh my, oh my, how dare such misconduct and the wreckless carelessness of these departments or institutions be shown to this young duchess? Now, if we think in terms of, ermh, how many years the stresses, the effects, and the inconveniences a bill like that costs, God knows. I guess she is the one who know how to talk to her father better. Allow her to write her own check. She be like I'm a daddy's girl. Really not the biological daddy. I had the vision when he tried to rob me from the bank. He was dressed as Gandolph from *The Lord of the Rings*. I had donated my money when I had my first episode to a children's charity; God knows I needed to hide some of my winnings, and God knows I am an angel in heart. I'm not greedy. I am greedy. I want all that I long for and desire, and ain't no one going to tell me that is wrong because I bring joy beyond praise. If you actually pay attention to what I say, you will know, and I know that that means I get served first. It took God to sacrifice his son to save us all. I've been sacrificed way too many times, and I am the daughter who has gone the extra mile here. Yes, I am throwing my voice and hearing as this sounds in my head as I write, but I write the truth of how I feel and what comes to me in how I expect the response to be. It's 4.18 a.m. I need my eyes to be hurting looking at the screen in pure darkness. I'll get to the breakdown of how I ermh disperse my own personal investments via my family, the one I was born into first and raised up with the world already robbing me. I telling my story. Even the doctor tried to tell me a few days ago, I'm, not ermh, what is it realistic to be a prime minister? I thought to myself, mother fucker, please, you don't know me. But on a level, something said you don't need to explain ya self any more to anyone. If I was, or when I am, my whole family and friends will be the new cabinet among those that apply for positions. I did write it down: how does one manifest to be the first black female prime minister of the UK? I mean, when I think about it now, Kanye West has just been showing me an example of how I appear to others in this universe. I guess we needed someone to do it, as this girl listens to men, not women. Hahahah, that doesn't mean they are always right, emmmmhmm. I saw someone with a meme, and the man had passed out on the floor, and the lady called the ambulance because her fella was unconscious, and the ambulance asked her why. She said it because she said he was right. I have to go. I have to go. I know not really, as God will give me the energy to sustain the day. God bless God's heart. He is so kind, loving, and thoughtful. I bet some kinda wandering really who is God. Like, nah, no way. This gally gally chats so much sh*t. I mean, you ever talked to your longest best friend, Theresa, who told you she could chat nonstop? It's unreal. Knowledge fascinates me so much that it irritates others once I find a topic to talk about It's like, oh my God, that girl could chat for England literally, and I actually never thought that would, you know, manifest like that.

I have to put it kindly when I say what I say. This chick knows how to put it into reality. Is she truly trying to touch people's minds? What really is the secret to manifestation? Ain't no one listening to this why I can't be in school teaching students can drive me crazy. I got to be in the right frame of mind me tells ya. 4.27 a.m., still writing. It is Erhh. December 3, 2022, started writing the book on Monday. We are nearly getting there not sure how long this will take me, but we are at around 9000 words. I wonder how many she is going to need to get through this book. I mean, if you saw her first book, *My Mind's Eye*, I thought, is she serious about these errors? She thinks that my mind is not allowed to have errors in typos from trusting technology to do its things, who says a passage can't repeat itself to make sure you are paying attention, and who says it must be presented this way. I am the author of the book. See you soon, angel for the daughter I do not have yet, or possibly me, not sure, but it is an investment firm in my family. I will see some angels soon. That book may be the making of me. I mean, it sold a few already, and I am not going into the hospital again. I said that was my last hospitalisation for a reason. They wanted me to help them with all the patients because I was the only one who understood them. I said to my husband, I'd like to be a doctor of psychiatry. I understand a lot; I'm gifted. I can diagnose by just pointing and stating which area in the book, depending on the obvious condition, etc., what is going on. People underestimate spiritual situations and healers. But I tell you no lie, every single person that has been around me has mystically and miraculously transformed their lives. I ain't saying that, that's me but God does his things always divinely.

OK, people, hello again. It's me, Duchess. 24 January, and I'm still going. Y'all was going to know when I'm did once the books in your hand. But it will take a few guesses to try to tell how long it really took me to write. So I've been manifesting well, putting things into reality, and activating the potential possibilities of things I'm trying to achieve at the same time. Last night, I had my celebration of my new Letitia Antoinette handbags arrive. I had my neighbour over with her fella. It was amazing. I actually got a chance to load all the things that I want to manifest in my life or that I wish I had tried. I came to realise how I hold so much excitement inside of the things I long to do. I fear that it will get talked down or ridiculed, and no one needs those types of vibes. So, I wanted a new handbag collection for this year, and I made it happen with careful planning and by just doing it. I kept researching till I could find a manufacturer that would do small batches of customised bags. It took me six months to finally find someone. That's why I think I also went for it. Number one, I fell in love with the first image of seeing what they could be; second loved the way my logo looked on there; and third, hmm, they could do what I wanted with a small start or number in comparison to others. So, I do believe that you have to work towards the things you want to manifest. I don't completely believe that it is just gna va va vroom right in front of you because it passed your mind. I mean, that would be awesome. In certain situations, yeah, it may feel very much like that is a matter of changing mindset; everything else changed.

I still long to be a well-known musical artist and author where I can actually rely on a bit of income to be generated from that. This will enable me to spend more time with my kids. The new lip-gloss line is on its way, just waiting to sell stock before I venture there, but colours and designs have been made. I wanted to expand my network, so I returned to some of these clubs I was connected to see if there were others alike that I'd like to meet. Goodness me, it's like nine fifteen a.m. I think I am writing, but my eyes are getting sleepy. It is time to get a coffee in my system to wake me up. My vitamins alone are not enough; I need more, more, more.

It has been a while since I wrote about manifestations. Of course, I return here, as I am always trying to somehow manifest greatness in my life. So, I haven't given up on my dreams of being a world-star singer. I would still very much love for the world to hear and embrace my music and share my stories, just as I am here writing and sharing my very thoughts and emotions with you. I am getting to the next stop, King's Cross. I shall return to let you know how this manifestation has been going, so have a great day.

I shall be back. So I am back. Unfortunately, it is not possible to write in breaks, so I can only assume you joined the break as I was at work.

So, in the manifestation of artistry, I got myself back in touch with connections with people I made with whom we either started some projects or I was either too busy to be able to follow through wholeheartedly. I mean, with modern society now, you never know who you come in contact with and whose really talk or really walk the walk. There is a particular guy I came across on Facebook who is all about joining artists, promoting them, and setting up tours. I reconnected with him as I noticed the website domain I had set up with him had run out. Similarly enough, I also recognised it was around the same time we had been first in contact; it was cool. I shared links to my music and my videos, and he shared with me his banner for their upcoming tour. Before you know it, we were on the phone with my husband for a good two hours, and by nightfall, he was preparing my pitch for Universal and Sony. He believes I got a good few hits that need to be heard. Who knows? It may just happen. So that was my manifestation of meeting key people who can help support me to get to the next stage in my music career. It was nothing too exciting to explain, eh, but it made me feel good about the process. What do you long to manifest in your life, and who can assist and support you to get there? It's like, why waste time picking up the phone, making a few calls, and getting connected with the world out there?

So, I feel I should be in the manifestations chapter this week, the second week of February 2023. It is the start of a new week, and all we want to manifest is greatness, peace, joy, and abundance. Opportunities come within abundance itself. Somehow I've manifested myself to be on tour in July and Goa in April. I mean, these are the potential manifestations as the invitations have been given. Time shall tell if it is to occur. Just go with the flow, doing my best to remain positive.

So, howdy people, I hope you are well. It's 5.44 a.m. on Wednesday, 1 March 2023. I woke up to immense pain in my pelvic area, be it fibromyalgia or the ever-present pains of unusual periods, which affect women in different ways. I think I am experiencing the mighty pains without the bleeding, and it is so painful. But fear not; we are manifestations of the greatest pains we feel are usually labour in this area and that to bear the greatness of a human being. But I must admit my periods come defeating like labour contractions and are mighty strong, so whatever is happening through this period of time, I can only digest as great things to be born. So, I have started this New Year with the termination of unhealthy friendships and relationships, partly so I could focus more on myself and partly so I could be even more driven by myself. So I can experience the enjoyment and excitement for myself. Without the need to always share my exciting ideas, I can learn to keep things to myself. So I can learn that I know what others do to try to dissuade me of my plans and vision that are given to me. Because many don't understand me. It is not wrong to want a better world. It is not wrong to want to improve things. It is not wrong to want to train your mind to actually be capable of creating changes. So, last night, I returned to my creative visualisation meditations. But not too long before that, a recruiter emailed me to apply for a job offering a salary of £70,000 a year. I was so excited because I thought my skills and attributes matched this role. Or not so that I thought, as I wasn't looking, but the sheer approach got me wanting more. Then I saw another job appear on LinkedIn for £120,000 to £160,000 a year. I thought, well, that is surely even better than the first email. Why not go ahead and try to apply? What type of living would one be able to afford with that kind of wage? For my children, for my family. So I went for it. I woke up believing that it's time to action this manifestation of mine to be the first black female prime minister. It's like I can't even be, really. The country is going into a deficit of debt. Those who are struggling are only going to struggle more; bills are rising and food is rising. It is so hard to get affordable work, almost as if the sheer thought of hope is trying to be sucked away from humanity. If you can make a change, don't you have the right to put it to use to make that change? Even if no one understands your vision, you must do your best to at least try. So, first things first, reactivate your party membership and see if you can get in on the next lot of elections. See how that goes first. As prime minister, do you know what the first call of action would be to save the country? I mean, you have been trained from a young age to do the best for youth engagement in the south-eastern region of England. You have been trained to know how for the whole of England. I think I would do the unthinkable. Change this country to develop a potential new party or reform some of the parties, as I do with Cooperative, which is like a two-in-one with labour. My goal would be to create a social enterprise system. Social care is of the utmost importance to our well-being nowadays. People don't want to talk, people don't know how to talk, people have no one to talk to, and you know what? They are left feeling and feeling more and more of the world, which they can't fully understand because not every generation has integrated into the digital age. I struggle to this day. It would generate renewability and sustainability in the long run. Healthcare could become more affordable, education more accessible, and travel more affordable. People in important sectors are on strike because they do not have enough money and only so little time to be with loved ones. We are meant to live life, enjoy life, and not slave away without feeling its riches, let alone experiencing them. Everything we give comes back tenfold, and surely there is enough for great efficiency all around, with less crime and more love and justice generated. I am sure we do feel robbed by how justice tends to work here, too.

So, I am back here in manifestations, so I think it is fair to say I should consider another chapter specifically for goals. Well, goals have been written, and you notice it seems like I repeat some things in life. So, I am here looking at manifestations, not just in the thought of what one would like to manifest. But the results of the Midas effect on the actions that we put out there. I recently shared online about the success of my documentary '*Letitia*' and how it had been selected to be screened at the mental health film festival in Malaysia. I was in such shock. Of the positive responses from individuals, I didn't even realise people generally do keep an eye on some of the information that I put out there. Nonetheless, that action of working on a documentary led to me receiving an invitation to be a speaker on mental health and human rights in New York. I could not help but want to share that on my social network. I just felt like the universe was playing with me. So the thing to think about is that in life, we may want to manifest many things, and at times we may not even realise how or what that manifestation will look like. Not just that, but when it manifests, are you going to be ready to collect, accept, and receive what you tried so hard to manifest? Don't be scared. I sure do get scared of my own abilities to manifest the things I desire in life. When it occurs, it is like someone saying, "Please pinch me." Is this real? I'd like to manifest more of those pinch-me moments.

Relationships

A man can never understand what strength it takes to be a woman until he loses her. It is just the nature of the world and how we have allowed ourselves to be programmed to understand. There goes that saying: you do not know what you got till it is gone.

We women are the ultimate force that allows you to enter this world, thanks to God's divine plan. We women are given the ability, not all by God's blessing, to carry a girl or boy, which then grows into a man. We tend to naturally refer to God as he, not all, but most, from what I saw of my upbringing, dependent upon your religion, or if even none, then I can't speak for those of who you are known. But the awareness for me is God the Father, the Son, and the Holy Spirit. Nonetheless, the man assists in delivering the sperm to the womb for that foetus to be born. We women carry the whole development of a human inside of ourselves. That child chooses the womb it is released into. God knows what other processes occur when it doesn't go through fully, leading to a miscarriage, but the worry and distraught to the mother is delivered through affecting us in yet another type of way. Because a child was still present even if not delivered. And for those who abort the child's choice of you, maybe it was too much that they themselves were not ready or in a position to be able to do so. But it doesn't completely block another opportunity until the tubes are tied.

I talk through the distress of appreciativeness and disrespect of my standing as the strength of the woman I am today because we women have our morals and boundaries of what we tolerate, as do men. But through my own experiences, it is clear to see that it takes a hell of a lot more time for men to mature and actually have the strength of women to have to deal with their bullshit of the day. The pride that lies in men lays and sits differently for women. I am not saying we women are all the same. But we have a womanhood that appears stronger than men's manhood of actually sticking together.

Men like to be treated like children because they behave like children and endure recycling over the same situations time and time again with the need for guidance to step out of them. It really is a simple process. Just as a man is shocked the day a woman ever listens to them, it is as shocking to us women when a man finally decides to listen to us. Life would be completely strange if we all listened to each other now. It could definitely be much easier and smoother, but no. We humans need tension to keep the fire alive. As I mentioned in another chapter, the species of men and women in the human race complexes. But yet, it keeps us on edge.

I am not an individual who likes to argue, bicker, or stress. But I am also an individual who will speak up abruptly, strongly, and clearly when wrongs are being done. I am quite a justice seeker. I appreciate equality and respect because we are all born with mostly the same things. However, there is the rarity of some with two hearts, some with both female and male organs, etc. Yet, we are all special in our own ways. It takes a while for many to actually acknowledge how unique and fantastic they are that they allow negative vibrations to take control of them and seep through the ore of them that they let exasperate to every living thing around them.

Men like to talk amongst themselves about how we women are crazy. We say one thing, then do another. Yet they do the same darn thing. There is always a battle of the sexes. God help you when it is the same sexes because it is even more like a battle against your own self when coming to an understanding because of how our hormones are behaving. The truth of the matter is that people lack patience and empathy, and most are selfish or selfless. There just comes the time of the explosion when the only place to release it is the one that is closest to another. That is the so-called better half. But not all the time are the better halves in the mood for each other bullshit. When they know they have a whole load of themselves to deal with, like who wants to allow anyone else to come and disturb their vibe when they are flying high and doing well in life, and it is like, oh, you be feeling things about different, please don't put a downer on my vibes. You do what you can to lift them up, but you know the only person. Who knows best to deal with yourself is yourself. Time alone can drive you crazy; in the silence, time alone gives you the loudness of your thoughts. Time alone makes you think of all the other things you could be doing. Time alone is, in fact, the perfect time to get to know yourself and learn about yourself. Just because you're a teen in your twenties, thirties, forties, fifties, sixties, seventies, eighties, or nineties, you still discover things about yourself. You think maybe, in the later stages, you have the gist of things. But time has a way of also reversing or reallocating your mind to a different time of yourself so that you're completely away from the present time. That then leaves some misunderstandings for those around you because they long for the you of you now, not the you of you then that they hadn't met. But such is life.

We can only do so much for each other. That the ten per cent, the ninety per cent is you in yourself, and that, my darling, can be a whole load of a lifetime. Men and women were born to be together so this universe can continue to reproduce and recreate, which is the natural science of reproduction. We would not exist without that. Yes, in modern times, scientists are doing their best to make changes to go with the trends and desires of society. Who knows? I don't.

When I talk of relationships, I talk of my own experiences of relationships, be it relationships in marriage. Relationships with work and relationships with extended family and friends. But the overall relationship as a whole is to relate well to a ship that sails. So many have been sinking because they allowed water to fill their ship, weighing it down. Washing away all the goodness that made you all so relatable to one another.

So, how is your relationship? Is it good? If it is not good, how often is it not good? What is it, or why do you think that is? Do you believe it is solvable? If so, how? I mean, a therapist really does not do that much apart from giving you the time to talk in a justified way and entering the pauses when it's necessary to listen to each other. It wasn't cheap, either. It's like, how on earth did you ever even become one together? I'm sure if you think about it, you could laugh at some of the stupid things you did together that brought you to each other. Memories are our riches of gold. When those good memories fade, you almost always become old. We are always forever youthful at heart if only we allow ourselves the time of day to enjoy ourselves and the company we share with each other. So that's where the patience comes in. That is where the gentle heart swings in being there and being considerate without judgement but with empathy. The difference is that one can't pull another out of their own self-pity, but one can give them the space to do so. Yet some are so scared of that time alone that they get lost in what on earth to do because they become lost within themselves and have forgotten who on earth they are.

Relationships are not about forgetting who you are, because we mostly fall in love with a person for exactly who they are and how they view and live life. But that changes with their very selves because of the battle they face with themselves. Suppose you refer back to the chapter on the species of demons we face. That may highlight that area more. We are our own worst enemy. For what reason?

I can't say that we women are always right, but as women, I am going to say we are. So, space was given to the drama of the day, and the better half was still available to be able to listen to the issues that one faced throughout. At times, there is no need for explanations as to what occurred, but to be able to be there to comfort one another because of the silence, and in the holding of one another, each other understands one another's heartbeat of emotions that they are battling through.

Not every relationship you hold in life is good for you. Some are bad, and some are good. Some nourish you, and some provide support to help you grow. There are some that simply try to bury you with lies, toxicity, feuds, rage, and procrastination, and you have to break free from them. I broke free from a relationship—a so-called friendship, as I call it—through a simple reveal of wrong words spoken, which came out in the wrong way. It may not have been meant in the way that it came, but theory tells me if something was perceived in that way, that is exactly how it came out negatively due to the energy and arrogance released within it. I took it upon myself to share it with a third party involved as they were the subject of discussion before I knew it. Insults were thrown. A truth revealed revealed even deeper buried truths of their ugly disregard for me. I can only control myself, my thoughts, and how I feel. I can predict how someone will respond due to the traits they have shown and what is known to me about my understanding of them, and they walked right into it. The way to release yourself from bondages and relationships that don't serve your higher purpose can be, at times, to be the match or add fuel, but so gently, without even needing to open your mouth directly towards them but near them. Hatred is a stench that shines out loud from a person's own vile words that they choose to use. They will hide it well and mask it with fake words of support, but they will always bring up the topics that are truly masking, such as I'm glad we don't compete with each other, meaning deep down they are envious and want what you have. Deep down, they are vexed about how you are getting what you're getting, but in your eyes and your ears, they are telling you, "Well done, it's awesome. Your biggest hater at times is indeed the person who hangs around closest to hear the latest news like an eager vulture." Needn't worry. God protects you from all angles, so always keep your heart pure and your intentions pure. Because those that are not for you will always be revealed in the divine timing that is relevant to your growth and succession. Breathe easy and be humble in all your endeavours, even when you are aware that your actual relationship or so-called friendship is actually with an enemy at hand that comes across as a true frenemy. A frenemy is a person who befriends you when they can see which benefits they can potentially reap just from the very essence of who you are. Do not be afraid of anyone, as fear gets us nowhere. Yet fearlessness takes us out of our comfort zone and into the unknown. There are yet many relationships to be experienced, and the most important one is the one you hold with yourself. Do not allow yourself to tolerate garbage too; tolerate rubbish too; tolerate negativity too; tolerate people's dramas; tolerate others' insolence. Focus on what makes you happy, what makes you laugh, what brings you joy, and what takes your breath away in a good way. Which fills you with inner peace? Wishing fills you with contentment. These things cannot be bought with materialistic things at all. But yet, time was spent and gained with one another. There are much more things in the world that unite us than separates us.

Relationships take time to work and flow in unison, mainly due to the need to understand each other's timeline. Most issues occur because of imbalances, and to gain balance, time is needed to endure to be able to ride out the hurdles or obstacles. Quite often, I come across friends whose issues within their relationships tend to be because the fella won't do certain sexual things. That is the going down on a woman, I say, talking if anything, but it is OK for women to go down on a man. We don't get to openly discuss about the whys a man wouldn't want to yet, along with how to enable him to want to. It is part of exploring each other's bodies. Embracing one another, being able to be vulnerable, and opening yourself to each other to have that ultimate pleasure. The reason some can't, I believe, is because of their own limitations and set beliefs. No one ever needs to know what sexual things you do with your partner, apart from the parties involved. When you resist giving full pleasure, it is ultimately a refusal to submit. There is a blockage and an imbalance; it's a part of the individual that you're choosing not to understand or connect with. When a woman gives birth, she gives her all to a man through her acceptance to carry life through and within her. Not all men understand how much of a queen a woman is. That is why we are patient and understanding. I am not sure scientifically where it started; I ain't going in that deep. But it takes a longer journey for men to fully comprehend women through our different hormones and states of mind. Yet, men, you're not always open to expressing what's in your heart as much as y'all can be great listeners. Relationships hold so many angles in terms of how they are formed and how you get together. Yet also how you spend the time you have together. It is in bonding and being together that we learn. It is in being truthful with love and compassion in your heart that you're able to understand how another feels. Wouldn't it be perfect if relationships were so swimmingly aligned that most of what you experience is elatedness, joy, laughter, happiness, passion, and none of the frustration, anger, disappointment, annoyance, or insecurity? But I guess at times, we need a mixture of the ups and downs so that balance can be achieved. Some people give up very quickly on relationships because of personality clashes and a lack of patience to get where the other has come from. Quite often, it is forgotten that the other person is also an individual with a past history, which makes them perceive and internalise the things they do the way they do. How much time is truly needed to fully let a person in? How do you know that you're ready to let them in fully? Why do we restrain ourselves from fully opening up? Is to protect one's heart from a barrier allowing one in. Or is that caution because the soul is sensing something deeper and that maybe you're not truly aligned with the right person? Questions: Do you fight, persevere, or just move on and focus on yourself? Quite often in marriages comes that hurdle at times, but it is the very vows I believe that lead you to reflect upon yourself before you haste with rash decisions. It also brings you back to the centre as to how and why you joined as one, as that is not a decision that comes so lightly. As for single individuals, it is a very different story. You may have kids you are managing alone; you may have a career you are focusing on; you may have experienced past hurts as to why you are now single and still focusing on yourself. You're like a butterfly in a cacoon, munching and digesting the very bits of how the person is opening up to you, and the digesting is you embracing the parts of themselves that they are opening up to you. But you can only break free from that cacoon until full acceptance and ignition of the relationship ready to go full bloom have awakened. So be patient with yourselves and your partner. Beauty takes time for the love that's to endure for a lifetime.

Dreams

Dreams most have some most don't. Dreaming almost feels like fantasies about what you long to experience in the future. Sometimes, I sit on the tube and watch all those posters and signs of artists lined up as headliners performing. I was thinking did I give up on that dream of being an artist, or should I keep going? Technically, I became an artist, just not as big as I thought I'd be, so in hindsight, it was still an attempt at a dream, a goal. Sometimes, dreams pan out much differently than what we envision in our minds. They occur in a different way. Or we just lose hope or check ourselves into a different reality and are like, fuck it. I'll try to do something else, maybe in that field or something else. Most tend to say artist managers are usually artists who just gave up trying for themselves and kept going to help it happen for others, as they tended to discover so much along the way. GPs are usually surgeons who couldn't be asked to keep going, etc. I do not know for sure just what opinions I have come across.

Sometimes, we sleep and have a dream that sends messages to us about things that have occurred throughout the day. Sometimes, we pray before we sleep for answers to appear in our dreams for guidance for the day ahead as to how one should proceed. They say, well, some say it is good to have a journal beside your bed so you can record the messages. I tend to use my phone. A lot of information can be downloaded while we sleep. God knows it is a rest we are meant to wake up from. But that does not always occur for some. Are you sleeping in life or dreaming your life away? Do the things that make you happy only live once? Yet many claim they have been reincarnated. What did I come back as?

I remember having an episode when I felt like I came back as a dog that was sandy in colour. It is like looking at the reflection of a window, and that is what I could see. But generally speaking, I always wanted a dog. I'd name it Sandy like in the film Annie; however, in these times, I can't look after a pet.

I was talking about dreams yesterday, and little did I know that even I had forgotten what my dream job was. Because there have been many. One of my dream jobs was to be a complementary therapist—an actual complementary therapist working within the hospital, helping people with cancer and terminal illnesses. I trained for it for a long time, and little or often, I wouldn't even get through to an interview, possibly because I hadn't had experience working in the field in a hospital. But had plenty of work with people with terminal illnesses and end-of-life carer's privately. I decided to believe in myself last month and kick myself in the butt, not literally but in the mind. I decided that if I wanted something, I needed to apply myself better. I mean, complementary therapy positions only started coming up regularly more often after COVID; before, it would be every two years or so, and they'd only be volunteering positions. I trained for three years and spent thousands of hours volunteering. I did a lot of volunteering in my training years and a few for those with disabilities later in Barnet's career. It is different to support people in the hospital in comparison to working in a spa or a clinic. The appreciation level is different, and the needs are different. I am not in the position of lying in bed in a hospital to fathom and understand what they are going through, but I have compassion and empathy to know that I honour the body they lay in and will do my best to alleviate fear, anxiety, and pain the best that I can through the power of touch. It warms my heart to be able to be there for others so often; it is just hard to express what we feel.

I struggle so much to let it be known how I feel that I just write and write and write. I felt that I had also reached my dream as a successful international award-winning artist; when my fans finally started approaching me on social media, what touched my heart the most was being told I saved someone's soul. I may not be well known, but my music has travelled, so I have travelled across the world without even leaving the UK. Through my music, I touched people's hearts.

So, having reached some goals makes it feel like dreams are possible. I guess it's just us ourselves that fail to see most times that we are living the dream without realising it instead of just thinking about it. I also dream of owning my own home. That feels like it will now be a possibility with my new job. However, they gave me an offer the new job of pay, and I was like, yes, that's great, but then I slept on it and thought about it and was like, hmm, I'm only going to get one chance to get this right. Ask them for a pay rise now as they went with the second best option, not first. I remember coming in second in my beauty pageant for Miss England when I was younger, and the way the crowd roared, you would have thought I was the winner. I was second best, then, you know what I mean, but it felt like I was the winner. If, for some reason, the winner couldn't take part, I would automatically take her place. My dreams, goals, and aspirations have sometimes felt like near misses—so close but just not quite there. Something definitely is in the air this year, especially in the lead-up to my birthday—new blessings, new beginnings. Now I need to tell you about my most recent work that I am leaving because better has been given. It is like staying in a role that has a higher, tighter, and possibly quicker route to progression. Whereas, like, only staff is contracted, and everyone is casual and manages that team that, in a sense, seems so tense when you are around. Yet they are showing you have been with a company for years and have no contract. Or go into the private industry for a job that you trained for, specifically one with much higher pay. In these situations, you can clearly see money talks. Not just that, but the institution has much more structure in place, with the funding to care for its staff and to develop their stamina. My other long-term dream is to become a doctor in psychiatry. I already inquired years ago about this and was advised I needed the counselling qualifications to be able to, regardless of my postgraduate papers. This is something I will still consider for now. I wonder how I get on the property ladder upon employment, as that dream was to be owned by thirty-five. I cleared all my bad credit by twenty-nine after entering an Iva when I was twenty-two. Careful planning does the trick. Even my husband is strangely considering my ideas. I guess I am smarter than I think without realising it, but I did once upon a time believe I was a genius. I'll leave that for another time.

Have you ever woke up from a dreamlike, yeah, yeah, that dream reached out to me? I am going to change my ways and my habits. Take a new leap of life. I am that person today. In my dreams, we were in great discussions about me becoming an athlete again but actually taking it seriously to compete, not just for the fun of it. I mean, every time I go to the track, I see this girl there training, and she starts talking, saying we have to train. We have to give this a go. Why not? We have nothing to lose. But somehow, when I run on the track, I run in lane 1 and end up in lane 9. It's like, how am I not running straight? I could see the track. When that kept happening, I decided to change my technique and move into long jumping. *I thought, yeah, this seems much better, but the run-up to the distance I jumped just seemed so miraculous that I was jumping to the edge of the board and flying.* See, I take it as, oh, when I get to work, I must train in the gym and, when the weather is better, get myself on track. I used to love running with the wind in my hair and the wind in my face. Feeling alive—oh, the freedom—was beautiful. What is this newborn feeling like coming out of me? I like it. She sounds fit as a fiddle. I went to bed at ten p.m.; it's now twelve thirty a.m. I feel like I had all the sleep needed for today. The dream workout got me so pumped and alive. But no, I am going to reign it in. It beautifully snowed outside. I wouldn't say it is deep. I say that England's weather is deep, meaning maybe kids aren't going to school tomorrow or trains and transport must stop. We have never been a country overprepared for snowy conditions, so give out the weather alerts in good time. But it snowed earlier than predicted. It indeed looks like a snowy Christmas. God knows if my party is still going ahead; I do wander through all these preparations. My friends do have a crazy streak of spontaneity that quite often shocks me. I just saw one of my dearest friends on Facebook with a Mexican hat on in her slippers and scarf dancing in the snow. I like, yes, girl, why not? She did bring joy to my eyes. I guess I am going to go back to sleep. God knows what else I will discover in my sleep. If any dream analyst picks up a different understanding of my dream, do let me know. I sure appreciate it.

Battles

In life, we all have some battles that we deal with. The battle to get up each day, the battle to feed ourselves, the battle to fight addiction, and the battle to not harm ourselves. The battle is to be better. They are all battles. Like I mentioned earlier in one of the chapters, my hardest battle has been the university trying to fight my case about how mistreated I was. Being a vulnerable individual with no representation, the hits come as fast as a blink of an eye. I lay in bed to myself, thinking about how I should die. Should I drink all these chemicals in the bathroom and pass out? Then I snapped myself straight out of it. I was like, this is not how my story ends. I have a life to live. I have children. I wouldn't dare want them to ever see any harm come to me as much as they had to live through the experiences of me having been sectioned and taken away in the ambulance for my own good. Those things you don't just forget can have a worrying effect. I felt disgusted by the lies the university had said about me. I thought it would be best to talk to God, so I prayed for him to take all my worries away and lighten the burden that I was facing. I prayed that he would relieve my mind of worry and hold me close to feel his presence. I said that I was grateful for all that he was doing for me. For the opportunities that he is preparing for me. For the blessings of my children and my husband. For the home I have for the restoration of health, and God knows physically and mentally, I am always battling, but he has been working on me to be better. I said thank you for everything and that the devil is a liar. I saw the attack from the university and was coveted by all the goodness that surrounded me. My dearest friend Mary gave me guidance as a friend, my non-biological sister, and rest assured me that it was time to sleep. I was so grateful for all that God had put in place to prepare me for the battle that came and went. Amidst the situation of discrimination and victimisation from the university.

The biggest battle is in how you react, and being vulnerable every millisecond counts. You are not your thoughts, and at times, I feel medication kinda makes it easier to seep in if not at the right dosage. But it was strong faith, hope, and love that pulled me quickly away from taking note of the thoughts.

I mean, what has been your worst battle in life? How did it make you feel? Did time feel like it was standing still? Could you actually shed any light on the situation in real-time? It was difficult. Before, my battles were dealing with my child in school—well, not being in school—and trying to keep him connected to education. It helped once the term passed to have him back in school, but having been away from peers for so long, as a parent, I had to protect him from his battle of rejection from education temporarily as much as I could. Sometimes, you don't realise that the battle is part of the pressures that help you overcome to level up in life. Levelling up is your growing strength. The endurance and stamina of perseverance. Running for long periods of time in a cross-country I've never done a marathon, but life pretty much feels like one at times. Up and down, up and down. Having bipolar, they say your moods can be like extreme mood swings, but you know life is bipolar in just as many strands, as one day from the next can be two entirely different things. Is each day ever the same? How could you identify an identical day? Or is it technically the day, and everything canvassed of the day is the same—that it is your mind or soul that is ever-changing and searching? I am not sure you know, but I guess everything does have its system in place of how it should be.

What is your outlet when things are not feeling good? I mean, how do you deal with it? Some tend to release anger on others; some destroy themselves without even realising it. Until they are forced to release it. Just like a fire that expires, you can't avoid its heat. Well, unless you have magical powers that avoid it, but I only see that on TV.

Another battle is not as much like the other, but it has my skin and my eyes. My skin has become sensitive, like suffering from eczema, which I haven't suffered with since I was like twelve, and now there are regular styes in my eyes. I don't know if you recall how I mentioned Louise

Hays's book *How to Heal Yourself*. Well, from that, without actually looking in the book I see skin sensitivity in relation to the Chinese year that I was born, which is the snake, as a sign that my old skin is shedding off and a new part of me is trying to reveal itself. I see it as something physically obstructing my view of life, and the clearing of that is still in process. You are not able to see as clearly through life until the bumps are smoothed out. Quite rightly, in my life right now, I am feeling those processes. My body has entered into a new job role, which means a new routine and new time patterns of sleep, rest, and activity. Another job is trying to prepare under that, and it is hard to see clearly exactly how the paths are going to be as there are so many other protocols in a process that need to be seen, which may be the little bumps. So sometimes, yeah, the physical battles are in relation to what is situationally occurring, but that is just how I view things. To try to make sense of things. That is not to say that I don't need to go back to the pharmacy and get some drops for my eyes because the irritation is bearably unbearable.

All right, all right, all right, so I have a few battles that I have been fighting. It is my own mind's thoughts. At times, I punish and torment myself and push myself too hard without realising it. I started a new job and have been adjusting and adapting to the new surroundings, new people, and new processes, internalising everything. Yet I get anxious because I am on probation. I took my medication for pain, as training in the gym kinda aggravates my fibromyalgia. It is like trying to do better and be healthier, but your body can't handle the growth of changes to strengthen it. It is still early days. Hopefully, the pain will ease, but I have taken so many medications that it has made me hyperactive and worry even more. I somehow managed to calm myself by going outside for a walk and getting fresh air. I was shocked by all the people that were outside. Working full-time, I guess I start early. I do not really see as many people in the morning. I felt like I had been so out of tune with the world—too much TV, too much resting in myself, and not socialising—that it felt overwhelming just to be outside amongst people. I believe in the battles yourself; it is very important that you can understand when things are changing and affecting you and to have a strategy that helps you to remain calm. I am not saying this happens to everyone, but anyone can expect anxiety attacks even without medication. I just felt the need to share that because it was a battle I overcame. Not only that, I think it played on my mind to let my manager know about my condition, as it was not shared with him even though he was my manager. But for me, it helps to have the person who is guiding me aware so they understand and can be supportive. Which I am truly grateful for. So yeah, it was some kind of day that even I couldn't believe, but we just got on with it and lived life. Be proud of the things you can achieve and of overcoming battles. The biggest battle we face in life is ourselves. So be kind to yourself and look inside your heart.

At times, we battle with our old self and our new self. Quite often, when you find that peace in yourself, it spreads to the rest of your life. But even within that stillness of peace, some old traits of characters that you used to tolerate slyly try to creep in. But because of the lessons you learned in the past, it is much quicker to shut it down. My kindness used to be so much of a weakness to others. I allowed myself to let people have easier access to me.

With the digital world that we are in now, it is so easily achieved. If it is not a phone call, it is a text; if not a text, it may be WhatsApp, Telegram, Facebook, Instagram, TikTok, Snapchat, email, or even a website, or whichever other platforms you exposed yourself to being on. These are all doorways of access for some to peep in on you, study you, etc. I am that person who learned to block delete as a means of peace of mind and to prevent access. Because if they can't access you, they can't trouble you. They can talk amongst themselves, but you needn't care about what is said behind your back. Some even realise that depending on whom you're connected to or how they were connected, they will have the audacity to reach out to another to try and find the reasons. Doing nothing is enough of a reason. Sometimes, people are in your life for periods of time at different stages of your life. Life teaches us through what we go through individually to know, value, and love ourselves a bit more. If it has not happened yet, it will occur eventually. Don't be scared to speak up for yourself. Don't allow others to make you feel uncomfortable. Allow people to bring joy to you, help you better yourself, and believe in yourself. As a light worker, I very much stand out as a sore thumb to those who are troubled as a means to help. But the most important thing is also to protect yourself and not allow overly negative energies to drain you. You must have your limits and boundaries set if you're to keep your spirit free. Pain is too heavy an emotion to hold inside, let alone channel it to others. It is great to have compassion and love for others. That is where the love of oneself is so vital to one's own survival because your survival is another person's manual in how they get through, as we are all connected near and far beyond.

One of the battles I hate is my health. By evening, I can't feel my legs numb and full of pain, just as my arms and hands are. Medication doesn't help, apart from trying to meditate to trick my brain into not thinking about the pain. It is not fun. You can't even call out for help because, well, the very vibrations to raise the voice just feel too much on the body. Speaking of my health, that was the physiological side. I find the psychological battle tiresome and straining. One can't help but be an overthinker and an oversharer at the same time. The repetition of situations is tiresome and daunting. They are definitely daunting. Recently, I have been struggling with the shock of extreme fatigue and exhaustion. My body just wants to shut down, and it does not seem to matter what supplements I've taken or how much rest I get. Nothing recovers the energy except to ride it out. It leaves me feeling guilty within myself that

I am so tired that I often forget that it is a part of the symptoms of fibromyalgia. Some think I have so much energy. How do I manage to do so many things? I guess I try to take advantage of the energy I have when I do have it because when I'm shut down, it is a horrid battle, and I have no insight as to how long it will last. It helps to talk out the emotions with my husband, who is so supportive and understanding, but then I still can't help but feel like a pain in the ass because I am complaining about myself. When what I should be doing is trusting the process that my body needs time, not guilt-tripping and mentally punishing myself for my own symptoms with negative thoughts, it just triples the tiredness, if that is even possible. So yeah, I do feel it all happens for a reason. I try to remind myself when I like that of the fact that, like, well done, you got up and got out of bed; well done, you got up and went to work. You didn't call in sick; well done! You survived the day, paced yourself, and slowed down when you needed rest. Yet now, on that return home, you can enjoy quality time with the family. When one has battles or difficulties, it is important to be able to not have to keep these things to yourself, or your own anxiety is going to eat you up. I do this to myself often, and it is so soul-busting. That is the importance of truth in all things. Being able to be truthful about situations will slow the burden from being lifted, which will enable you to feel lighter and less conscious of thinking that everything you are doing is wrong when it is not.

I Am

I am powerful. I am loving. I am love. I am my own solution. I am motivated. I am strong. I am successful. I am bountiful. I am beautiful. I am flowing with life. I am releasing all negative attitudes behind me. I am moving forward in life. I am comfortable with new changes in life. I am positive. I am divine. I am delightful. I am humble. I am peaceful. I am tranquil. I am full of energy to fulfil all my desires. I am hopeful that today will be a great day. I am prosperous. I am abundantly gifted. I am intuitive about my own needs and those of others. I am empathetic. I am persuasive. I am skilled. I am creative. I am clever. I am inventive. I am an innovator, and my new ideas come to fruition. I am love. I am gentle. I am wonderful in all my endeavours. I am beautiful inside and out. I am trusting and loyal. I am determined to see things through. I am resilient. I am tenacious. I am bubbly. I am fun and joy altogether in one. I am in control of my emotions. I am confident in all that I do. I am hopeful in my faith. I am divinely protected. I am courageous. I am strength. I am a bright light, shining consistently. I am highly favoured. I am fruitful. I am harmony. I am my own heaven. I am intelligent. I am honest. I am truthful. I am calm. I am energised. I am invigorated. I am my desire. I am sweet. I am funny. I am open to the adventures of life. I am as light as a feather. No worries can touch me. I am of a large harvest. I am happy. I am well rested. I am indestructible. I am incredible. I am ambitious. I am brave. I am charming. I am magnetic. I am exotic. I am free. I am grateful. I am glorious. I am good. I am happy. I am honoured. I am unique. I am insatiable. I am irresistible. I am responsible. I am friendly. I am a leader. I am a good listener. I am understanding. I am patient. I am considerate. I am merciful. I am surprising. I am astonishing. I am overcoming. I am relatable. I am forgiving. I am pure. I am enchanting. I am respectfully respected and respect others. I am special. I am one. I am wise. I am content. I am fulfilled. I am assertive. I am disciplined. I am devoted. I am smart. I am generous. I am prosperous. I am wealthy. I am healthy. I am adaptable. I am rejoicing fully. I am flourishing. I am enthusiastic. I am indispensable. I am decisive. I am not my mistake. I am incredible. I am interesting. I am an overachiever. I am prepared. I am amazing. I am indulgent. I am faith. I am sincere. I am infinite. I am the essence of joy. I am a breath of fresh air. I am elevated. I am surprised. I am humbled. I am deeply rooted. I am transcendent. I am a soul connector. I am a spiritual healer. I am a money-maker. I am opportunity. I am a star. I am beloved. I am a believer. I am conscious. I am ever-changing and everlasting. I am a dreamer. I am my greatest desire. I am eloquent.

Sight

I don't know where I was going with this chapter. As soon as I wrote sight, I deleted it. Then, something stepped in and said no. You must continue this journey of what sight is. It's importance. And how it falls into restoration. I guess there goes the saying, "Seeing is believing," not for all but for most. The sight brings us depth into life, depending on how much you see. Even with the naked eye, you can see a lot more about a person and a situation than you care to see. I guess that is foresight and sixth sight.

You ever just know. Maybe someone is not good for you from the get-go. But there is just no opportunity to break free. Once you see an opportunity from afar, you make sure it is the right one and go for it. Sight can save you so much heartache in the long run. But only if you act upon the reasoning that has been placed in front of you.

So I return to sight as I begin to see more clearly the road ahead with a better understanding of the path I've been taking. This path led me to remove all distractions, which made me feel like gossip. Fed my ego or led me to try to discuss personal feelings outside of myself. Sight allowed me to look inside myself because it's so often when we see that people may be in front of us or accessible because of sight, it is an easier means to reach out to them. But yet, when you do try to reach out to what you can see, it may not be the response that you expect. That is why, at times, it is better not to have any expectations to avoid any disappointments. Any response, you should be grateful for the effort made, even if you are not satisfied. Sometimes, they are not paying attention to what is in front of them because sight is so easily taken for granted. So often in life, we do not realise what we have until it is gone.

Sight made me look inside at who I am. Why have I been lost? Where has all my time been going? What did I enjoy about those that were in sight? When did the negative emotions grow? Was it on the things that weren't in sight? Take away the judgement of everyone and everything you ever experienced, and put yourself back there. Do you still feel the same way about a situation or person when you take away all the judgements and just see them?

Sight can lead us astray of ourselves and of our very loved ones. Because of how we materialise the sight of which we are seeing. Do you know what it is to have sight but sight of just love? I much preferred that way of life—enduring the endless forgiveness of wrongdoings and being able to move forward. Sight teaches you to place boundaries for your own stability and balance. Sight shows you that we all long to be comforted and loved, regardless of how miserable we may appear at times. Sometimes, we do need the distances, but the out-of-sight, out-of-mind is true to a certain degree. It does not mean that you are out of the heart. Sight is experienced in different ways for some. For those who may not physically be able to see directly with their eyes, they still have sight for life and can see what life is all about. Sight is of the senses, and how in tune with all those senses are we? Could you listen more? Could you speak less? Could you taste it all? Could you smell the vibes? You feel vibes, so how is your heart seeing, or do you listen? I can't recall the voice it makes. I recall that it is the very best thing keeping us alive.

Miracles

How many miracles have you experienced in your life? How long did it take you to realise it was a miracle? Instantly? Momentarily? Or as the years passed by?

My husband and sons have been my miracles in life, as has a lady named Grace, who came bearing great news. I remember in the early days when I had my traumatic experience of being swabbed for DNA by the police. I was numb; I was in shock. I was feeling less.

I remember going to the studio the following day and speaking with my now-husband. He asked, "How was my weekend?"

I said, "It was great." Had been kidnapped, and God knows what else, to be fair, didn't want to go into it. But I spent most of the night in the police station; it was atrocious.

My now-husband turned around and said, "OK, are you OK?"

I was like, "I'll be OK."

"So what are we playing today?" he replied, and we went back to singing. I felt a golden light shine over me and over him as he calmly played so gently, giving no mind to the ordeals I was talking about and feeling so relieved that even he did not want to get into what had ever happened but focused on the time we were in. For me, he listened to me without listening so effortlessly that I felt at peace. I knew then, had I been blind, that this man sat in front of me and has been around all these years, and I only see him now. That should have gone into the previous chapter of sight. Sometimes, you realise what is in front of you when you lose it and get rid of what is not meant for you.

Sometimes traumatic experiences are the only way to escape from situations that you shouldn't be in. You may not see the bad things as blessings at first. But it sure was a part of the person I became today.

So he was my miracle one. My second was my sons. If it wasn't for my children, I wouldn't have become so fearless in my will to strive for life the best I can. At first, so many were disappointed that I was becoming a mother because they saw me as having big goals and big dreams and having gotten so close to becoming Miss England in my early days. I mean, I remember the judge asking why I wanted to be Miss England. I said because I deserved it and strutted down the catwalk in my diamanté ball gown. The crowd loved me, and when they announced the winner, you would have thought it was me who had won, as the applause was so much louder when I got up on stage. I took myself into labour and had an emergency C-section. The changes I experienced through carrying my firstborn born were that my working hours were chopped in half because my work colleague was bullying me, expecting me to lift heavy weights while heavily pregnant, etc. I had to be moved from the athletic centre to the golf club. It was just around the corner from each other, but at least I had the golf cart to drive on. Some of the customers would try to teach me how to play on my shift. True, say I never ever returned to try to play. But it was a tough pregnancy. I wanted to get married while pregnant so my son wouldn't be born out of wedlock. For some reason, I believed it was very important for a child to be born with the parents' wed. It is like a form of protection in my eyes. Nonetheless, I struggled financially with my firstborn, both working part-time, and money was going low. Bills were soaring high, and well, I spent a lot of it in the hospital because I had a thing called an irritable womb. I was a very petite person, and couldn't handle the growing pains of my oldest. We had to have an emergency C-section, as my long-time mate had said castor oil helps to bring on labour. I mean, it does. I just did not know how dangerous it was. I drank about half a bottle. Of course she forgot to mention you; just take a spoonful. Then I started feeling some tweaks and eeks. I had a bath and then felt more pain. The only person I had at home with me was my now-brother-in-law Maly, and he didn't speak much English, as Polish is my husband's first language.

I remember calling Maly Maly to help. I was in labour. He looked at me as to what on earth she was saying. The only polish I could remember was *Zadwon* Daniel

Zadwon Daniel *Teraz*. He replied by calling Daniel. I was like, *Tak! Tak!* He called, and somehow, the ambulance was on its way. My husband ran all the way from work to get back in time for the ambulance. My mum was stuck in traffic. God knows how she got there, but before I knew it, we were in the hospital. They had put the monitor on me to check my son's heart rate. They said, "We needed to get an emergency C-section because his heart rate was too high." I think the cord was around his neck. I had to get him out quickly. Straight to the theatre, we go. Only one could come in, so I brought my husband. I had to sit as still as possible as they injected the spinal needle in my spine to numb everything so they could cut him out. 17.17 Tuesday, 8 February 2011, my baby Romeo Luciano was born. Don't ask me the weight. That is his daddy's thing, as he was forced out with forceps, then my husband cut the chord. He was quiet for the first minute, then roared out a little cry. He looked like a boxer from where the forceps had been placed when he came out and straight onto the breast I fed him. I did not move an inch that night; I let him lay on my chest till he fell asleep.

My second born was, oh, so different. It was a natural birth. But boy, oh boy, I always do what I can to get them out early. I was exercising, trying to keep busy to get Casanova Giovanni out. This time was very different because I was self-employed, so I had more alone time while he was brewing inside. I wrote *Little Star* one of my Christmas songs, while pregnant with him. Labour was ridiculously long, thirty-four hours, to be precise. I started getting the contractions in the early afternoon, went into the hospital, and kept asking to be checked. They were like, you have a long way to go. I had been in the pool gym ball, and by the time they took me to the delivery suite, I was with my stretchy band, which you pull apart and breathe in, then breathe out as a means to manage pain. The doctors were so fascinated by how I was managing my pain with this band that they went into discussions about it while I was in labour and actually were testing the band. I'm there thinking, *Hello, I'm in labour here*, but I needed to keep the focus on my breathing; I had my gas and air. Had my waters broken, for I had pethidine, and then there was some other medication I took by the early hours of the next day, which then meant I couldn't feel a thing? I regretted taking it, as I lost the sense of feeling as to when to push. I only knew to push when the midwife would tell me to. But that is what happens when I listen to the advice of others. I listened when it was my baby shower. My friend said, "Take everything they offer you, even if you think you don't need it."

So I did. But by the time my Casanova arrived and that last push came, I was so full of adrenaline, strength and excitement. I literally felt ready to do it all over again. Never did I know that pain can be liberating and empowering and that you can concur with anything. That was the feeling I had with my second child. I did later go on to experience postpartum psychosis four months later.

There was definitely was a shock to my body in accepting the new womanly figure and the hormone releases that I experienced with my second in comparison to my first. That was a whole new ballgame.

My sons have also been miracles in my life because of how they changed and shaped me into who I am now. Every part of them, which I carried to how they are in their day-to-day lives, has equipped me and fuelled me to have the strength within that I have now. Love is endless, unconditional, and infinite. It was like my firstborn; I experienced the sense of disapproval of becoming a mother, and my second was the disapproval of naming my son Casanova.

With the first, I was battling a lot in life with situations, people, and injustice, while carrying my second. It was a lot on my terms and flow of things, but the final hurdle was the battle with doctors in exhaustion. They were adamant that I wouldn't naturally deliver my child and wanted to give me a C-section, and I was arguing while in pain that that was not about to happen. These sporadic conditions fuel me differently to stand for what I know will be.

The differences between Romeo Luciano and Casanova Giovanni were that Romeo was out of wedlock, and Casanova was in wedlock. Romeo was christened Casanova; he had not been. When Romeo was born, I returned to work within several months and didn't have many outside agencies involved with support. When

Casanova was born, I had outside agencies involved. The health support worker pressured me so much that I went on medication. I took sertraline because it gave me hallucinations that, for me, I believe, contributed to the postpartum as my physical body had never ever taken medication to deal with one emotion. It was already a shock to my body, having delivered naturally. By the time I was hospitalised, I thought I was being punked in that program jack ass, as if someone were playing a big prank on me. It took a while to digest what was actually happening.

My children are my miracles because they are every part of me. I can't envision my life without them. To have had days and nights away without them without my choice was heartbreaking enough.

My first ever miracle in my life is my mother, for her unconditional love, sacrifice, and devotion to raise me and accept me as I am, even when the world is against me. She has always helped me to believe in myself. Of course, she drives me crazy, but I love her even more for being who she is.

New Year

So the New Year has arrived eighteen minutes in, and I already had to pick myself up from a gentle disappointment. I saw my mates had gone clubbing for New Year's and thought to myself, *Why ever do they never invite me to join? Simple; it is just God's protection.* Not everyone you know always likes you that much. It is time for you to rest and be with your family. Enter your new chapter peacefully. Those were the thoughts that turned around the feelings.

This year, I truly am a new me. I've been feeling the excitement for a long time. Well, the last few days purely because they come with a new surge, a new feeling. Friendships have died, and a new part of my blossoming. I took myself to the gym today to prepare to strengthen my body so I have the health to meet the demands of each day. Not only that, but also as a means to help get me to stop smoking. If I choose a healthier way to get healthy through participating in exercise, perhaps that will counteract the need for smoking, and it will make me just automatically stop the changes I will be feeling. I want to be more alert and manage situations better instead of letting situations manage me. I want my view of how people treat me to become so defensive, thinking everything is an attack from afar. Even if perhaps my instincts are right, I will trust that but rise above it.

The sooner you're able to replace negative experiences, feelings, or sensations with positive ones, the sooner and easier it becomes to maintain a positive mindset constantly and consistently. It will be just like breathing. I am happy. I am the happiest I've ever been in a long time. I feel good, I feel strong, and I feel peaceful. I even treated myself to new hair into the New Year, so in the morning, I don't recognise myself because I fully went for a look I not had in a long while. My children and husband are well and healthy and so happy, which brings me joy. Listening to my youngest tell stories out loud in their room. My boys can tell stories for days to delay sleeping. Bless them.

This year, I started my new job and joined the gym. I want to finally pass my driving test, as I have seven months left before it expires. I want to change my whole wardrobe of clothes now; that is a mission that could take a whole year, with the seasons and all. I was going to join one of these women's social groups where you pay a membership and go places with women. However, I just missed the fifty per cent discount. I am sure there is something else out there that is not as expensive. Really and truly, socialising is fun for me, and it is not fun at times. I am at a stage where I believe I need to be alone. I get so easily afflicted by others that I need to spend more time with myself. Friendships aren't really my thing, as much as I love people. I find myself only managing to be in them for a few years or months. I prefer no heart aches. I have my family. They provide me with a lot of love and joy. I literally spend more time with them and have more adventures because they are who I want to spend the rest of my life with. Not those that seem so few and temporary. I want to live without regrets. I do not want to see myself needing to go to the hospital or to see a doctors for any type of condition. I want to release some music throughout this year. I want to stand firmer in myself. I felt proud that on the last day of last year, I had already started implementing changes such as making a smoothie instead of junk food. I can't wait to discover new parts of me. Self-discovery is fun. What do you look forward to? We shall survive.

I seriously can't believe another year has gone by as quickly as it did. I can't help but feel anxious about it. Changes come in so fast, as do blessings. I think I generally think and worry too much. I really wish the worries would disappear there, as unhealthy worries are. I guess it leads you to the unthinkable. True, I need to collect my cake tins from my neighbour, who said they drop em back once they finish with them, but they have not yet returned.

Hustler

A hustler, to me, is an entrepreneur with a flow and steady moves. That knows which vibe they are in. I mean, today I randomly started the launch of my new handbag collection by Letitia Antoinette. I haven't gotten the bags manufactured yet. I just have them drawn up with designs of how I want them in all the available colours. With my name stretched out over them, I will be so proud of my name, meaning to bring joy beyond praise. When I see people rocking these new handbags, I want them to feel joy beyond praise in their own lives, in their own way, with a spring in their step because they are amazing in their own way. We are all unique individuals, for sure. That is the order I go: I hunt, I find negotiations, then mock of the products I want, promote, get the feelers, purchase, and get the manufacturing. The revealer receives and then does what I have to do to sell. Holla at me, brand ambassadors: first, my girls have priority in new product orders or potential new clients, then it repeats. As time passes, and depending upon my other commitments, I then have to be like, hmm, we need to place this in the boutique to let it sell while I try to earn elsewhere. If, throughout the year, I see stalls, I'll go to them. This year, I am going to work more on TikTok live videos of products, as I feel so different about these products.

So, like I was saying about the hustler, it's three fifteen a.m., an early first Thursday, or January 2023. I woke up early, full of life. I get back to sleep eventually, but my girl got worse to type out and a book to complete. I need to let you in on my process. Because I am trying to utilise my maximum time for my abundance and wealth. Productivity is key to process progress. God, even I don't know where this side of me has been hiding. I think I am a hustler, baby; laugh out loud. You have to be street smart and people smart. What is it that is going on out there in the market today? The media tells us there is a living crisis. You see, in the stores, food is expensive, and it is just rising. You go into the superstores; it's forever a sale and loads of stock, and I guess prices are high too. Social media shows more and more in the comfort of their homes. Cosying up to their own paradises. That is not the case for all, but we are all survivors in our own way. If you are reading this right now, we get from A to Z somehow. Even without thinking and realising it, we are. It is just like Nike says, 'just do it'.

If you need something to achieve or something to do, do it. If you want to improve your life or your situation, just do it. It really only feels long if you let yourself think about it. But you get on to it; rah, that much time has passed. Look how fast it is that time has passed since you became an adult, became a parent, became independent, got your steady job, watched your kids grow, now have your own grandchildren, etc. Time is feeling like an illusion out here. When you realise there isn't that much of a guarantee that you have each day, you start using your time differently. I think we can be in Hustler for a little while. I only touched on my hustle when it comes to products, music, and loving family. Jeez, that is another ballgame altogether. I work in quality bursts at flows that feel right for me, so I have to bounce and get myself back to sleep; I still have work in the morning and work while I sleep. The way I will be trying to process ideas in my dreams is to remember and jot them down. Like, do we truly ever switch off but forever rest in our days? It's too early for questions. *Alie, night, night, morning, beautiful people.*

So, good morning. People hope you are well. As I would like to reiterate, and you may notice throughout chapters, it is like a disappearance from one to another; that is indeed so. As they have different topics, different parts of me and different areas get activated over one another from time to time. So, one of the things I enjoy doing that you may notice is actually capturing my real-time experiences and thought processes in how I get from A to Z or A to B. I said hustlers are about flow with steady moves. In order to flow and be steady, it comes with great consideration and contemplation of things that are working and things that are not. I guess also, in other words, the hustler is partly the characteristic traits and components of the entrepreneur. So, I have been reviewing my most recent venture of preparing handbags, overlooking my potential future investments in more gym wear. But the mind tends to want to oversee and drive more so to the ventures that don't need so much of my physical time so I can focus on full-time work. As we know or may not know, the digital world relies very much on the automation of life and the algorithmic processes of people's attitudes and behaviours. Will they buy this? Will they like this? What are they engaging with? What was it about this content that kept them there for so long? Being able to look at yourself enables you to help master the skills in how you observe and digest the way others respond to your products of creativity. So, for a good few years, I spent a lot of time by myself as I created content or did lives from my phone. The purpose of these was to act as video therapy for myself so I could recognise what I looked like when I was positively attuned and be proactive in maintaining that. Then, when it can happen from time to time with a condition without a condition, life knocks you a bit, and you need to pick yourself up and reconnect with yourself. In my experience, it was going into manic episodes, which, in my own beliefs, were spiritual awakenings. Once I have gone through the institutional processing of being in and out of the hospital, trialled from one psychotic to another. By the time I came out, it was a shock. It is a shock to see how home feels a bit like a stranger because you are not always completely out of choice and have the choice to be away from it. So your body's not been forewarned of what that experience could feel like. Oh, things have moved and are here and there. You have been away from your roles. Not only that, the effects of certain medications have readjusted some things in your mind so much that they feel like a blur. So, I always say it is important to know who you are to be able to bring yourself back to yourself. Quite often, having a mental health condition and being neurodiverse, as it's also called now, side effects, drive you away from that. I've always been a naturally healing person when it comes to the mind, but because I was experiencing another side of me that was viewed as abnormal by others, I had to be open to testing and trialling new medications because we always want to be better within ourselves. Well, I do. The point I am trying to get to is that it took me having to be the true me, which is stubborn and disobedient and prefers some reason to learn the long route to understand. What works for me is being active, being in nature, and talking out loud to myself. I mean, it is a natural thing to do now; in life, the main person you see on the screen is yourself. And also being comfortable with oneself. Little did I know that I was recording these contents of my processes of thoughts and feelings and my self-exploration of noticing patterns in my life. When I returned to the videos, I was like, oh yeah, that makes sense. Even I can relate to myself now because knowledge is timeless. Quite often, we say, if I knew what

I did now, then things may have turned out a lot differently.

Things turn out perfectly the way they are meant to. So my point, I guess, is that sometimes you don't realise the greatness of the very activities that you partake in life. The ideas at times relay in the background of your mind, oh, I want to do this; I want to do that. Quite often, it is pertinent to keep a lot to yourself and channel it in the most appropriate way that works for you. I'm sure you don't want to be working every single living day of your life to survive the very affordable abilities of life. But I would very much like to enjoy the wanders with ease and without worry. I do delay getting to the point of things, but I'm not writing an essay to be marked against criteria for approval any more, so the concisions are not going to be endured as such throughout. I shall return in due course about the weighing of options and the implementation of options.

Entrepreneur

The entrepreneur is an individual capable of putting their ideas into fruition. They are able to look upon their own skill set and resources and utilise them to the best of their ability so that they can earn from them.

My first experience with entrepreneurship started at a young age. Entrepreneurship is something that we can be born with, depending on how our ways have been conditioned. When I was younger, in order to earn pocket money, I would do a deep spring clean of the cupboards in my mum's kitchen. You can imagine the mess seasoning makes when on the shelves, and many of them. I emptied the whole cupboard, washed down the shelves, removed any expired stuff and replaced things neatly and tidily.

Being an entrepreneur is more than just putting your ideas to fruition. It is a lot about knowing who you are and having the willingness to learn about yourself and work on yourself. I'm not on about surgically working, but you know, for some, it may be the case of a new body, a new persona. It is what works best for you. I've always had the mindset that I like to earn from the things that I enjoy doing, so it doesn't feel like working as such. But more than just being within your purpose, When I became a mum at the age of twenty-one, returning to my part-time job and being away from my newborn were two of the hardest things. I missed out on some of those moments of the first words and first steps that were witnessed by staff and his father looking after him. So, I took it upon myself to retrain in a trade that I believe is always generally in demand: complementary therapy. These were times in the UK when university degrees were about to triple in price, so I made it just in time. I studied part-time, worked part-time, and had a loan from a family member to pay back all at the same time. It was tough work trying to raise a little one at the same time, train in new skills, and earn. But you do what you have to when you've a family and your goals to fulfil. It does matter to have willpower as an entrepreneur and belief in yourself. Being able to visualise the potential outcome even from the very start amongst all the obstacles you may face or be facing. So, I guess the ideal word is optimism here. Being able to know what type of learner you are is key to your success, so it is always best to get an analysis when you start something new for a better understanding and insight into how you learn. Preparation and having the key tools enable success not only as an entrepreneur but also in most things in life. So, I learned from being practical that auditory theory tends to be my weakness, so this course suited me as it was very hands-on.

When you're deciding upon what it is you want to specialise in, take care to understand the course structure.

Also, ensure that it will be enjoyable. I, of course, enjoyed being a massage model throughout. Nonetheless, it is a trade I have stuck with throughout. Through my own life experiences, I've always been a person who likes to learn how to do things without reading the instructions first. Going by sight, then going back to see where I've gone wrong and implementing those changes.

My first official business position was as chairman and young consultant in regeneration and renewal for the south of England at the young age of fifteen. We were a social enterprise, so we would have our base fee per hour, and when being hired by different government departments, we added the additional fee on top that would go back into the business. Now, depending on the aim, goals, and purpose of your business, I have always found that social enterprise is a great method for ensuring the sustainability of a business. Nonetheless, the downside can be that you initially need a budget to work from. We had received funding that got us started, and I believe part of it was personally funded by our CEO, Jane Brooker Wood. God rest her soul. She sadly departed a few years ago. It was an experience being so young to be given power and support to enforce change. Challenge the people who were decision-makers to listen to us and enforce our recommendations. It really taught me a lot overall. We were all known as young advisors. Long story short, when the funding ran out and everyone that was in the team started to go their own way due to study commitments, as it was not too far from the age of finishing high school to college to university, there was a wide range of ages amongst the group. I took it upon myself to start on my own as the foundation of young advisors. I was so excited when I got my business bank account opened. Little did I know that they did not set up the account correctly. I was sold a free business bank account but was getting charged right away. While having no income coming in. I kept the contacts that I gained during my time as a young advisor. But because I wasn't necessarily the person who got the contracts and deals through, I had no idea where I was going or what to do.

Entrepreneurship, at times, means putting yourself in the deep end. You're bound to get into flight or fright mode and figure out how to swim out when it comes to trying to survive. If you don't try and don't make mistakes, you are unable to gain lessons to learn from. I learned that you need structure; a plan helps guide you as to where you are going. It also enables you to identify your weaknesses and your strengths. My strength was courage and the willpower to try. It is in doing things that you learn, not in sitting and doing nothing.

Incapacitated

Not having the capacity to decide for yourself and make decisions is not an easy place to be. I've been there. We are going to delve into the depths of exactly how it is not always a temporary situation for most.

Often, when an individual is having a nervous breakdown, psychological manic episode, or psychosis, they lose the ability to think clearly and decide appropriate actions for themselves. Even to themselves, they may feel that they are capable of it, mainly due to the fact that their mind is somewhere else. In my experience, I felt like I was in a different realm, experiencing and hearing things in real-time, yet no one knew what I was on about, and it caused great concern.

I talk about this because it was a temporary situation. This book is about restoration. As an individual with bipolar disorder quite often, it's dismissed what the effects of hospitalisation can cause. Nor is it ever talked about or support truly given in how you return to the normalities of life and the effects it also has on your loved ones.

Acknowledging one's experiences and overcoming situations is key to restoration. Yet this realisation can take a long time to occur, especially if you have to adjust to new medications. It's very much a trial-and-error approach onto finding what works for you. It can happen to the greatest of people: the inability to be able to think for themselves and make decisions for themselves through no fault of their own, generally caused by stressful situations, lack of sleep, substance abuse, or bereavement. Know that things can get better. Also, to not be ashamed but to accept the ordeal one has gone through.

The best practice to prevent such occurrences starts with you. Learn to view yourself in a more positive light and make the necessary changes that positively influence your life for the better. Be it a healthier routine, a smaller circle of friends, or new work, prioritise what means the most to you, and work on yourself little by little. Learn to be kinder to yourself to get through each day.

I remember the first time I was incapacitated, in the year 2016, a few months after having my second-born son. I experienced a lot of hormonal changes this time around. Mainly due to the fact that I had a natural birth. I remember arguing with the doctors during labour because they were so adamant about me having a cesarean. I was just as adamant not to. I had gas and air, pethidine, and the other drug, but I can't remember what it was called, to help block out the pain. I had been in the pool and in the room rocking on gymball, but he eventually came out. The realisation of my new womanly figure felt like a shock to the system. When I was placed in the room, I was far away from everyone, and then one night, the doctors came and took my baby away, fitted a cannula, and gave him antibiotics I never even permitted him to have. Later, I came to realise that they had mixed my son's blood, and he did not even need to have the antibiotics. It was quite stressful. Upon being discharged, I had the health visitor constantly visit. She kept pressuring and pressuring me to go on antidepressants. I really didn't want to go into them. I mean, I've suffered from depression in the past, but never did I ever take medication to deal with it. I just always kept active and exercised to keep my mood up. But this time, the moment I ever took medication, it was sertraline, and my life changed. I began to have hallucinations. It was like seeing everybody with a demon gremlin looking beside them. When people would come up to me to hug them, I was scared sh*tless, but for some reason, I was so devout in prayer that I trained my mind to only fear the Lord aside from the things I was thinking I was seeing. All I could say was, Father, forgive them, for they do not know what they did wrong. I felt like I was having a very intense relationship with God. He was my every thought. Then it dawned on me that I must keep on with my previous career in music. There was a music conference coming up in Atlanta that Beyoncé Knowles's father was attending, and there was the chance to have a one-to-one meeting with them and perform. I was getting in touch with DJs for radio interviews, arranging meetings with property estates of places to rent should I decide to stay out there, jobs for interviews so I have work, and communication with my cousins out there so a place to stay whilst I go for my interview. I was buzzed, excited, and ecstatic. I was posting nonstop on social media. I generally tend to share memes of posts that I see. Then, one day, my aunt and sister came to my home unexpectedly when my husband was not there. They had bombarded me. Saying, don't you think it's too soon to fly? I thought no, then when she was talking to my aunt, she told me to sit. I was like, I'm in my own home. I can stand and move around in my home if I like to. One thing about me is that if someone is concerned about me, they have to come at me the right way.

Well, generally, I never see many families, so it was very concerning, and I felt vulnerable and intimidated having them in my home with their own accusations of me being inappropriate.

To cut a long story short, it means a lot to have family care and be concerned for one's health and well-being. You may not necessarily see it as that at first, but more so as an intrusion when the general contact is quite limited naturally. Nonetheless, I appreciated it; it was just that the approach was not very patient-centred or focused. It is sometimes easier to listen to a stranger or friend than it is to listen to family, as it can feel as if they are just interfering and being controlling.

I went into the hospital in 2016 for the first time now because of my personality and being naturally such a prankster. I actually thought I was being punked. After the first twenty-four hours of being put inside, I was like, yo, what am I doing here? I need to go home. The different characters inside were so strange and unusual. Randomly talking to me about things I had no idea about. I thought I was in the Big Brother house, some kind of competition, and that well, the stars were helicopters and planes of people from all over the world trying to visit me as if I was some world-known star that even I didn't know about. It especially didn't help because the hospital is an air route, so you regularly hear the aircraft passing by. I had all the different wigs, hairstyles, and clothes of mine there. I often confused some of the patients with how I transformed my looks during the day. It was fun for me. That was one of the symptoms the family had noticed. It was like I became a big girl who missed out so much on fancy dress-up. Before I was taken in, I was wearing my wedding dresses, my beauty pageant dresses, my tiaras, and testing out different wigs. Parading around in my heels, God knows what I was going through, but I was in elation. I hadn't slept for five days straight, and the more time passed, the more energy I got. I felt like a superhuman. I could dance all day. I even managed to do ballet. I'm not too bad at that when I release all inhibition and let go. I never knew it was possible to possess so much energy. Then, when I was in the hospital, I became like a boxer who was nonstop, training anything to burn away my energy and then singing. Oh goodness me, I would also sing nonstop, and thankfully, I was in tune, being a singer and all. The very start of the mania was my prayer. I felt like I had risen up to the sky's skylight and spoken to God and was having a full-on argument with him, complaining about why we had not reached our dreams yet and asking God to let my husband have his dream fulfilled so I could focus on the kids because it is safer for him to travel instead of me. In my mind, I had truly awakened to the realities of the world. I ain't going to go too deep into what I can recall in my mania state. But I think you get the gist of it definitely in a different realm.

Thankfully, I have a sense of humour and can understand why it was so difficult at times for my mum and sister to take me seriously and contain themselves from laughter. I'm quite a character. I mean bright blue hair, a big fox jacket, and size ten trainers. God knows what happened to my fashion sense while the onset of mania was occurring. But I tell ya one thing: natural labour has put you through some changes for sure. They later diagnosed me with postpartum psychosis.

So yesterday wasn't the greatest of days spent drugged up in pain, unable to do anything. I woke up to sudden pain in my buttocks. It was excruciating. Nevertheless, I forgot I had been diagnosed with haemorrhoids. My mind never really digested the ins and outs of what that was. I know that it now can cause a hell of a lot of pain. On top of that, coming to the end of my menstrual cycles, I was just going through the works. But even in my worst states, I feel guilty. I feel guilty that I lumbered in bed, guilty that I drugged up on medication, and just guilty that I can't do much of anything, and it is mostly genuinely me, the one with such poor health, that appears to have everything wrong with her. Such is life, eh? I tried distracting myself by trying to invite some people I know as distractions, but I got hardly any response. I think I'll just have to think about taking myself out. But I know I can't do that now. So yeah, it was a pretty shitty day, but I got through it somehow, thanks to the love and support of my husband.

When you wake up to pain, it is really not fun; it is so debilitating and inconvenient. With the horrid routine of medication after medication, you can't help but feel like a druggy. Timeless conversations with pharmaceutical companies to change your medications to something more effective instead of a cocktail that will eventually knock you out and tell you that you can't function. It's even more frustrating when you're such a doer in life that somehow you feel restricted and limited but have to keep a positive mindset and constantly adjust to what life is throwing at you. I noticed that physically, I got strong. It randomly collapses like a tiresome hill, keeps trying to climb, but then falls back to the start. It is a temporary feeling, to say the least, but the dreaded pain makes time such an illusion that it feels forever. I am bound again. My pelvis is causing me so much agony that pregabalin, tramadol, diazepam, and gabapentin alone just don't do the trick while the legs fall numb upon me. I have been trying to push back the pain by researching and focusing my mind on opportunities that have passed my way. A friend asked if I'm still running my record label. To be fair, I only ever placed myself and my husband on there through the many doors that wouldn't open, but I thought I'd create my own. In doing so, I achieved some success, but as time passed, I saw a lot in my body to be an artist. I also had another who wanted me to manage them. I saw this as an alternative route to somehow be within the music industry more intellectually than physically, as, well, my body can't handle it. We definitely will not be in this current physical state. But I can manage to work on the computer and help others achieve their goals while I focus on healing my body. I must attach myself to something to flee from the pain. If I don't think about it, maybe the sensation of discomfort will diminish over time. Nothing like mine matters. You really have to dig into that inner strength to overcome it.

Fire

Yo see me, but I always only allow myself. So that if I recover through it on my own way through all that you've known and how you do your own cover, Fright or flight, life or death? How many times have you felt the fire where you stand today? Where did that fire get you? How did it feel? Was it inside or out? How did you connect with fire? I express through my process of love the creation of expression experiences of life. Through one's own joys and trepidations about life itself, how much do you really keep of yourself for yourself and of yourself for others? I've never come across people not being able to stand themselves. We all do it in our own ways. Standing yourself, loving, caring for yourself, knowing yourself and every part of ya means, well, I believe you are in love and really happy, but you can get really mad too, but you don't go there in a horrible way. You emotionally regulate a sensation that isn't harmful. I guess loving, gentle, and warm laughter could be what's really bad about how you choose the context of what you'll digest and how you protect yourself from what you don't want. You aren't right.

So, fire is still about burning and soaring through the day. I got so pissed and irritated inside, I'm surprised I didn't get heartburn. So I go outside and breathe. I get so irate that I do not have the energy or air to exacerbate the need to explain myself. I tried it, and it made no difference. I say, you know, I leave one per cent for myself, one per cent I can't completely trust anyone, or I can't get myself back up. I know what it feels like for someone to physically try to stop you because they perceive it to be manic crazy, something they don't like without realising that it is scary to watch and hostile. You say these words calmly while it hurts your heart, but at the same time, you release the things that are not said because of a lack of fear or because of fearlessness. There is no need to tame a lioness in action whose energy of fire is not back down till you feel its heat. God knows which way. It will strike the words of purity; no filter is needed. I give you space to breathe cos I know you will need air to cool down, not water. We live in a household of fire parents, us, and air children, our babies. Opposite elements are so powerful and beautiful when they are all collectively in balance. Like a house on fire, and yet the parents are the ones who lead that. You need to be able to check on yourself at as deep a level as possible. Do you know how far back your lineage line is or the true traits of you through generations and genetics? What skills, what qualities, what desires, what ambitions, and what achievements were gained within your line or heritage, even just the passing thought of what if? What if no one gives a damn but you, that one per cent? Imagine what you can do. Jesus went for us, right? What greatness can you birth into your life because God burned you into this world to do great things, right?

So, fire sign, we deal with our negative issues in a positive manner. I was misunderstood by my husband. I spoke my truth, highlighted his hurts for me, and took myself up to get changed. I wore a lovely salsa dress with leggings and did my makeup. And just like that, a new person to deal with the rest of the day. We are always trying to be and do better. It really starts with how good you feel. I enjoy developing businesses, thinking, and drawing potential pitches so I can one day earn a damn lot of money. We all have goals when money is infinite. It's not all my worries go, but I hope they lessen, as I imagine there will be plenty to do and people to help and expand the growth of the world. Man, the excitement is phenomenal for what can be. I can't see it, but then again, I do it in the process. But trust people need to get in line and respect the Duchess as she is. I have my issues. We all do. I accept who I am. Not many accept who they are. Like God forbid, I told my husband what you could do when I went. I said, "Why don't you do something you enjoy doing, God forbid? I've no idea if he knows what he enjoys doing, but I wouldn't complain or behave like life wasn't going well." When maintenance is difficult to achieve, it takes one to minus their bitching and adjust their sight of understanding when a person is healing themselves. They were a person long before they met you. As one understands the times in which one has travelled, what age did adulthood truly hit? I left home at the age of seventeen or nineteen. It was more of an escape to be better and safer. Because the hold became unsafe amongst a sibling of mine. But, oh well, you move into the next phase. New responsibilities. Goodness, I drank so much water for my blood test. I got to hold this in such a long journey, it feels.

Fire and fire have difficulties listening to each other; they fire and explode in different etheric and metaphysical ways. But when one has already recognised the triggers and outcomes, it is able to guide a fire out to steady calmness and peace. But the rawness of the reach leaves them speechless, with deepened solemn sudden exchanges of understanding how significant her presence is that it will correct itself and adjust without you needing to tell them how. No one fucks with fire; it's horizon explores your every molecule, and it is despicable how badly they can cuss your ass down within a second.

That is how great the understanding is, but they realise it in time. But they need it done obviously in a gentle, taming way, as their hearts are full of mad passion. Weird right? I need to get to work. I may return later. Have a blessed day. But be proud of being a leader. Leaders lead and make more leaders. It is factual; there is no need to compete. I got one per cent, but imagine what can be achieved when the whole ninety-nine works flyingly.

Hey, hey, it's me, your one and only fire sign. I will always be writing as if you're right here with me, just waiting to see what I have to write next. Truth be told, should this chapter reach you, you should be reading or listening at your own pace. This may be the present time for me right now, but I guess I'm in the future of your present time of your arrival at this moment. Quite a fascinating way to look at things, if I do say so myself. So I guess you got it. I'm into star signs also, and I'm a Sagittarian quite often. Throughout, I've explained how I get misunderstood. Friendships don't tend to be my thing. People either get so close as to learn and hate as close as possible, then throw back in the face, blah, blah. The point I'm trying to get to is. It's vital that there be a cut-off point when people just stop having access to you. Boundaries are needed to protect one's own mental health and well-being. We have all these social media and social apps to allow people to view and peep at your life from near and far and have the audacity to want to stare and check-in. Forget about being human, sending a message to say hello, or picking up a goddamn phone. I'm through with that. I prefer to be non-conformist. I appreciate my privacy. If someone really is wondering why they've been unfriended or blocked on links, the last thing to go is the blocking of your whole line together. Suppose that is still there; there is a door, but unbeknownst to the humans of today. Technology controls emotion more than artificial intelligence itself. That is ridiculous. I guess that a typical

Sagittarian has to detach from others for one's own peace, tranquillity, and freedom. Don't get it twisted; I have a laugh to be among if the vibes are right, but don't bank on my greatness to entertain and keep things alive without anything to give. And what to give but time to show you actually value a human being, but hey, I also don't like pettiness; it's such a turn-off.

So fire and fire have erupted again, this time like a volcano, as it came to the realisation that one had issues they had been holding dormant and then chose to decide to share and release that while one was at their weakest and in pain. Now, fire signs have an unintentional, irrational way of letting things out somehow at times that just ain't great, but it has to be released. Or it burns them inside to hold on any longer. The relevance of the unintentional irrational ways is pretty much how fires come at you. They don't come gently out of the blue, but more unexpectedly out of the blue. Fires like to taunt each other without recognising them, taunting each other until they erupt. We went with the volcano because of years of history between these fires, and sudden changes and silences made them both become volcanoes. As the lava erupted, it started to cure the land and the foundation. The foundation for these fires commences on the day they took their vows—not the day of the first meeting or having a child, but of the vows. Fires are able to find ways to find each other throughout their relationship. It is easy to get lost in a fire so quick to be blinded that you need to be able to walk blindly with faith in your heart, guiding and leading you throughout. Fires will burn each other and hurt each other as a means of learning to survive, as they know that getting stuck in a fire can only lead to asphyxiation. When you can't breathe, you can't talk, and quite often enough, fire and fire struggle to communicate their emotions verbally, but through the senses around them as they walk blindly in their relationship, they are drawn together through their hearts, heat, and the beat.

Drunked Knights

So this chapter is called Drunked Knights—surprisingly not Drunkard Knights, as it took more than one person to be a knight. And the second knight has long let me, and we had so much of a good time that it's only Monday, and I don't truly know how on earth we are going to get through the rest of the month, but we are. And I know that I'll be on Triple Expresso tomorrow morning before it even comes.

I guess this chapter has introduced the drunked knights. Always tends to be in pairs. Deep down, I think oneself thinks it's safer to embarrass myself in front of one person than it is to multiple people. But it really was without intention to do so. But saying that and looking over how the night went, I think that alcohol actually does have a side effect on bipolar and ADHD now; that may seem obvious to some and may not be so at all. I think about it and how the topics of discussion came to a point, I guess, where I wanted to share my ideas, ambitions, and thoughts and my own embarrassing habits without thinking, oh my God, how will they perceive me now? I even shared how I think I'm a fart analyst as I like, well, not always like to smell my farts because, at times, my own farts do disturb me, and obviously, you can't run from your own fart. The smell lingers without me trying that. My husband goes crazy when he notices me trying to sniff my farts from under the blankets, and my justification is that I'm checking to see that I'm healthy. I even shared about my ambition to be prime minister, as I used to work in politics at a young age, helping to shape policies but saying it out loud more, so that was the second person I shared that with.

It's kinda starting to feel more like you might actually try to do so. Realistically, you need to have been in a party for several years and have a team that wants to vote, etc. But yeah. I enjoyed myself getting out of the house. I was anxious because I often know there is a big part of me that kind of does not know how to be in social settings, especially when getting to know people, and I think even more so women. I've had a lot of hurt from women. But yeah, time to sleep now until the next drunken evening. I left sober, but with a headache, so I need sleep.

Training

I ain't going to lie to you, but training really helps you get your sh*t together. I returned to training in the gym, going to exercise classes, changing my eating, and adjusting my mindset. You know what? I can't help but feel like I'm really training for my life. I guess that is the truth. We do train to live our lives even without realising that we are. Something has been telling me you need to prepare. You need to be strong mentally and physically. I mean, I've been feeling pretty much like a dodgy knee that keeps giving way, but I'm still pushing through. Something inside me says I must not give up. I must not give up on my efforts in my sessions, even when it is hard. And I must not give up on my life, even when the road is tough. I feel like I'm breaking into a song with those lines. I have been feeling a little anxious this morning. Being the first day of February, the doctors called me up on Monday to come in to redo my blood. I mean, he said something like, there wasn't enough blood to read the kidneys. I was like, OK, because the lady tried one day, then sent off, and then I had to return a few days later for her to get the rest, so maybe it wasn't enough. Nonetheless, when I got there today, I asked the lady why I needed to get these done again. She says I don't know, but then I looked at the form, and I saw the words abnormal. I think, abnormal lord, have mercy on my soul; don't come for me now with sickness. I can't help but be a little paranoid or think the worst because every day I work with patients with cancer, and, they tell me their stories about how they found out. It was just a routine blood test. It was just a routine stool test. So, I was like, oh, my God, I pray, please skip me; let it not be cancer. But at the same time, this training I have been doing really makes me feel like, yo, this is your time. Give it your all. Give it everything. No day is promised, which is the actual truth, but knowing that, we must still prepare for the days ahead. So, thinking right helps you stay straight, positive, and focused.

In the past, when I was younger, I used to take part in every single sport I could. I mean, I was always the fastest in school, from infants to junior to high school. I loved sprinting. I do the 100, 200, 300, 400, and even the 800 metres and some cross-country. I enjoyed competing, feeling the wind around me, and passing people pacing my body. You are so in tuned. I played netball and football as well. Training is about strategizing and finding a way to obtain the goal. 'You want to be a winner, be a winner', but it takes training, and the race is just you accomplishing a transition from one phase to the next.

So, what is your phase? Where are you going to? How are you going to achieve the ultimate outcome for you...of where you want to be? Do you want to get a better job?

Lose weight? Feel happier within yourself? I think we all know that the journey and the process of it all start with how we apply ourselves to our lives. We can do our best, and even if our best isn't our best, it always leaves room for us to be better than we were an hour ago. A day ago, a week ago, a month ago, a few years ago. But we are here at this present time. We are just trying to live life to the fullest of what we know.

The moment we are conceived, we are training all the way until the day we are delivered onto this earth for the rest of our days. We automatically grow inside to naturally become accustomed to our surroundings to see, hear, feed, walk, speak, and understand. Once we have that full development through loving support and guidance, we get on our way, and some pass that on to others in the circle of life. Yet sometimes, we become unaware of what we are actually training for in life. Just be yourself, even if you may not know what makes you. Sometimes, it is that exact lack of knowledge that makes you.

Self-Acceptance

Now, howdy people, I hope you are OK. God knows how long it has taken you to get to this chapter; either way, I hope you have been enjoying the read that has gotten you here. This book isn't written to be read all in one order, chapter after chapter, but to see how you feel fit to read each section. It's the same way in the process of how it comes together that I hope you find your way through it.

Now, self-acceptance is a bugger. It is relieving and comforting when you get to that understanding of accepting who you actually are. I've grown to understand that I'm, an individual who doesn't do well with having companions, or, in other words, friends. Apart from me, I genuinely appreciate being misunderstood. It is in the misunderstandings that people reveal their true colours to me—the ugliest side, the name-calling sides of themselves. The resentment, envy, and hatred. The realities that I've experienced with others have been hurtful. They stand out the most from the rest.

My good moments are with myself and the ones I love and live for. Growing up I've never been a person that stays in groups for long or even amongst friendships for long. I was the tag-along friend or the last-minute thought of whether you wanted to come. Not necessarily belonging. But belonging to myself is my own cause and purpose of oneness alone, where there is only approval of myself by myself for myself.

Later, as I grew up, I came to discover my diagnosis of bipolar, ADHD, and autism. I never realised how I am socially amongst others in a group unless intoxicated with some booze. I don't do well being aware of the attention that is coming my way. I even throw little party gatherings at my home when I couldn't stand to be amongst others; just to try to fight that fear of social gatherings. Even when in the company of others, I somehow find a way to keep myself occupied without even getting into conversation amongst them. I covered that up so well, I had no idea. I much enjoy and prefer my peace. I somehow managed to overcome others' scrutiny of myself eventually. But to overcome your own scrutiny of yourself, well, goodness, that's the hardest of all. I am my own worst enemy, as well as my own best friend. I much prefer being a best friend to myself than the enemy.

The enemy of me myself is cold, numb, constant, and excruciating, and it attacks the whole of me from the inside out. I've tried many times to run from myself, but we all know that's an impossible thing to do. You can't ever run from yourself. You can get lost in yourself, hide in yourself, or torment yourself, but my favourite of all is to love myself. Self-acceptance is being at peace with all that you are and who you are, living within the balance of everything that you're able to flow consciously throughout life. It's no good being a bystander and watching your life pass you by. I'm sure there are times we have experienced that. Or you're not ever truly sure where life is going, but you just keep going because moving forward is everything.

Self-acceptance is understanding the good, the bad, and the ugliest of yourself. Things that serve you well and things that don't serve you do no good at all. Being the owner of your life means determining which choices and decisions are right for you. Not being coerced by someone else's ideas. Making things a reality in your life. Overcoming crisis, battles, and struggles. Celebrating the wins, successes, and adventures. Never entertain the what-ifs, because there is just nothing you can do about them.

I've come to accept that I am a straight shooter with my words. They come at others straight to the heart, straight to the core, so raw that it irritates or inspires them to do better within themselves. Depending on how deeply they met themselves, I'm not an individual who appreciates dictatorship. I need the freedom to express who and what I am. I am an individual, a spiritual being with human experience. I feel everything as the empath that I am. Some feelings aren't nice, but I must endure the process due to what I've allowed myself to be exposed to. I am ambitious, I am confident, and I am strong. I am the epitome of disobedience.

So, it was like 3.05 a.m. on Valentine's Day, lying in bed awake. With the thoughts pondering in my mind, with my own mind and subconscious actually shouting at me, get the fuck up and write that chapter; don't you there ignore me now, or you ain't getting any sleep. So I guess that subconscious thoughts will also be my ancestors and spiritual guides tryna work through me to get to me in a way that is going to make me hear them loud and clear. This book is called *Restored* for a reason, because not only am I sharing my own restoration, we will be going through it step by step.

Self-acceptance, to me, is also the self-realisation, self-actualisation and self-awareness of oneself all in one. It goes deep, travels deep—not a five-minute journey into who on earth you are. Each year, we always discover something about ourselves. Sometimes, situations help you grow even if, at the time, they are feeling like they are breaking you. Now I know I'm not a weak person, but I am a damn right highly intelligent and intuitive person, as much as I second guess myself and my worth. It's like, come on, are you trying to tell me that you still have not learned from that lesson from how many years ago? Like how you are going to play yourself like that.

I lay thinking to myself why, why, what, what? Why are these so-called specific events reoccurring in your life? What is it trying to show you? Why is it happening to me? What is it I truly want? If God was literally answering your life-beckoning call, have you not practiced exactly how to get what you want and exactly how to get what you want to be given? I mean, she says she is a Duchess, always in demand, always in control, so sure of yourself, so why are you bitching out now? Hun, you did not travel this far in your life to get lost in the things you want in life. You did not experience five hospitalisations in your lifetime and even convince doctors that you're fine unmedicated to start letting any man start dictating to you how your life should be? Right, you did not spend nine extended years of higher education so that you could get the job of your dreams to just be flat out tired away from your kids to hardly getting any time with them to when your dreams start coming closer to try and decide I'm going to spend even more further time away? Nope, you did not. Everything everything everything in your life has happened for a reason. You are your own saviour in your own life when it comes to saving you because God has graced you with the gift of abundance, endurance, perseverance, gratitude, strength, determination, and purity of love to overcome. People see you and detest you; people see you and love you, obsess over you, and try to possess you to control you every single way they please. When you clock and turn away from what you see occurring, they go crazy, like, how the hell did she get away from me? You crazy. You have been labelled crazy in all kinds of things for always having joy in your heart above all things because the meanings matter. I don't know how your story goes, but you are the narrator who is carrying this and guiding it.

It may seem strange to you, but it is not strange to me. The best way some know how to get through to you is to get through to me because I am you, and you are me, and we are one. That's how the Lord is in my heart. He became my very tongue, the inner voice that speaks, and I learned a lot about who I am through him. Because God will teach you a way in which you will understand just how he will reach out to you to keep in tune with your purpose. Now, did I truly write in this section what I was thinking in my mind that was keeping me up? No, a wise man, my guardian, and my uncle told me you are not your thoughts. So, I just allowed the thoughts to guide me to express my heart's voice and what my soul was feeling. That has gone and done it now. I definitely feel awake and energised, but I have to go get back to sleep. My dreams are fuelled with much passion and desire. I have to get back and decode these messages that are coming in my dreams.

I find that self-acceptance allows you to understand your body even more. Quite often, the external stressors of life build up to be internal stressors in your body because of the choices you made. Ignoring them lets it build up until your body is so exhausted that you just can't function any more. I feel like I went back to my own bad habit of smoking. Applying a new physical regime of training weekly doesn't fully align with my path as a singer. I'm aware of this. I have been stopping and starting, and now I have the worst ever chesty sore throat. I rarely suffer from this. My higher self sees that as a sign from God, the universe, that I will metaphysically and physically let it be known to my body that something has to give. I suffer from my own choices that I make and have to be accountable for them. I'm trying for sure, but it needs to be better because it is painful. Yes, it is actually keeping me up tonight because of the pain of swallowing. Self-acceptance is knowing your own stubbornness if you have it.

Addictions

The hardest thing to ever own up to is addiction. It takes trying to step forward, repeating things, and recognising that things actually got worse the more I came back and returned to the same old bad habits. What is it that I crave to make me feel this way? Why do things that are going to cause damage? What is this so-called feel-good feeling? Is it just the raising of past emotions still floating as if there are today or traumas unresolved that you've not let go of? Who hurt you so badly that you want to damage yourself and block opportunities? Did you really say from a young age that you'd rather take the long road to get to where you desire in life so you know once you get it, you won't ever fall back?

However, addictions are generally associated with negative feelings and damaging traits. Why are there not parts of addiction that are viewed positively, huh? Let's change up the connotation of how one naturally perceives addiction. I'm addicted to working, to providing for my family, and to feeling good. Can you really ever have enough love when love is infinite? isn't living life addictive?

Well, it took me a whole few weeks of creative procrastination over Netflix and Apple TV. My God, like, do you understand how fun and great it is to learn about yourself? I had the most amazing few months within the New Year, and signs, signs, signs. I never even realised how I was building myself, just getting on with things. I pushed myself through my addiction to work to write a second book. Here we are, and we are two-thirds in. I go in when I need to; I applied for my training provider certification again. I don't know why, but I had to.

All right, so I'm back again. This time, I am sitting on the toilet. I am constipated. I am leaning forward with my phone in my hand. My other phone is just resting on the cabinet. I have my little CBD vape, so being addicted, I might as well be there in a moment of the strains of the addiction and how you manage things—are you gonna lie? I really enjoy having time to myself. I mean, I think we all have different sides to ourselves just through our traits and personalities.

I am attempting to use talk to type so much right now, and all I can see are the errors of how it's so slow to capture the words I speak in time. If you don't check these things, they sure have a way of making you sound so incoherent. I thought I attempted to make use of this because I go quite fast in thoughts; I want to do things manually the long way, typing that when I have time to even correct myself as well what sort of thing, so yeah, again, you learn it how you do things and be able to go back over that is a great, first-hand experience even quite often. Being an individual with bipolar dyslexia, ADHD, and autism, I kind of sign that it's like I have to do things in a certain way; it takes me a lot of time to digest things like that. It was a lot different from my living environment. I used to live really, really close to the train and just close to transport; just noise. You are always around this busy, busy, busy, busy, busy. All is the meaning of warning of an ambulance in the city as it's busy. You are; it's just like, oh my God, it's still noisy. I don't know if it is cool. Oh yeah, it's just the different contexts of the surroundings. It has an effect on the whole body, works the clock on things, and is very sensitive. Who is that? I'm hypersensitive; you will notice… This is a great swing of darts and mind my business exactly what I've been doing in London in minding my business. This is still the addiction section. Oh my God, I deleted, and I don't know, but the whole point of my timing on this is that it takes me that long to be able to get through to the point. That's another lesson that you're learning. If you need to know about distraction in life, not all the time, that's OK if you don't get the logic. Bring it back to myself, as I did a few weeks ago. I was saying that I decided I wanted to be on the board of a society. Now that I get to see this governance and your approval things, I'd like to say the first that I was talking about conflict and dealing with conflict with people. You can either be the type that is a conflict seeker and already have a leader, or you can just know you were the culprit in the sense that different scenarios are supplied. Where their less is more when you choose, unless it's more in your lights. What's gonna be the easiest way to get ahead if you've got the acceptance process in the early morning? Check a lot; it's just like what you're trying to determine in terms of efficacy, like ratios and aromatherapy. Learn about ratios. Phytochemistry is not a joke, and if you can try to understand your chemical balance in your body of work, so I don't work, and do you know and I mean, endorphins are good, love you, and good, good, good, good, good, good is one thing good to get. It is addictive after a while; it's just like, oh my God, you stopped, and it's like, I need a heck of a rest now. I have a lot of energy as I am looking. But you know what I got feeling within, and lately when I'm just going through this, it's just like I just wanna be myself, and it's peaceful, and no one says nothing. Do my work, do you go to see the people on your way, and it's little dosages of goodness opportunities of moving forward, so I'm cool that I am so bored with the story of the reflection I was saying, apply for this job. I want to be able to do accreditation things like this. I was like, in the past, OK, you were on scrutiny panels and things like that, but it just won't hold up here. Let's try to apply, but tell yourself, your inner child, what would you do—truth or dare? Oh, dude, just apply all through for you at that time because what happens is that when it comes to the actual interview on stage live, my kids are screaming in the background that you're in good communication. I am here being silent, but the balance in the house is showing me that energy is there. Are you OK? Because that's my love, I don't think I get it easy. I also need you to know that in part of this section, I attempted to use talk-to-text, which is clearly unreliable, so if parts of this section feel a bit puzzling, I want you to see the differences from when I was manual.

Personally, I actually never end it; I don't ever admit that I'm addicted to marijuana. Yeah, I like the chemical constituents of a plant. Would you find any food as well and seasons and episodes like *Little Helps God* in the winter, especially in winter as like, I don't get my feet touching the grass, the grass which charges me that was my little bit of grass but on a heated way I tend to walk in the garden of my garden to dance in the park or meditate. I do a new study by myself, an inspirational study for formative learning. All the study that was lying and detention kind of overwhelms me, not in the point of how many but also in the approach to try to get to know you on a personal level up close, what you all about type thing and then the walking away. Those hurts come near me to try to enhance the happy feeling that there is gonna be something about you that I might not like, and that's gonna upset those feelings. Align my time, maybe with my CPD vote, for something that is my alternative to Touch on WhatsApp on Street because there are too many things, so it's not healthy. I did get a prescription for private have to have CBD vape medicinally because I have fibromyalgia, and this one was more with the juice or something, so I can't give you for my actual physical pain because I have, so I found it online, and I just like you know this does the same thing for me is effective. I'm not having a go outside in the cold; it actually even pays me too much of it, so it's like I'm that addictive at times because a lot of the time it does not even come to the point of wanting a cigarette. I'm so new to my hands this movement ever so. Often, let me do that when you are able to replace that with something else to eat, and please write on. Usually, I would have it right in my hand. I decided to change it. Oh my God, my talk, so start Hello so this is the thing when you go on the line with technology to be trying to record your very dictation, and you can see how reliable one hour is in this technology because I want to be able to finish this book. It took me forty to do forty thousand words of creative writing and form. That's been generally the first lot was more fluid in a sense because it was like trading more so, and then as I got more into it, I discovered more functions that I could do on my phone, and I'm just like, OK, well, let me watch some Netflix downloading movies. I can't seem to find headphones, which actually kind of distracts me. I have been cutting my hair, and I'm going to give myself a haircut; it's needed. Goodness story to go into Lore Imene even discovered this year I lost my first voice call, close.

Environment

The environment in which you live is of great importance in maintaining and sustaining your mental health. This can be from where you live and also the proximity of your actual spouses. Those radiuses matter in how you internalise life.

So, as you see in the addictions section, the experimentation of ideas and ways of managing yourself comes through. These are processes of acceptance. These things cannot be achieved if you allow your surroundings to be surrounded by people who have negative connotations and lack hope in their lives, as it will affect you.

Depending on where you are, you may know your neighbours, but at these ages, you may just see them as strangers or actually never see them. It's important to protect yourself and be weary of what you allow near you or within your home, as this can have an effect depending upon what it is they carry within their hearts.

Even the environment in which you allow your mind to take you is vital. The states vary, and it's healthier to remain in the more cleansed state for better productivity of one's time and energy. I say it is healthier because I often allow my space to be cluttered. Without necessarily meaning to, but in a sense, my own thoughts feel cluttered and not so easy to release in clear expression. I guess my environment is, at times, a representative of how I am feeling inside. It makes sense to me where my mess may be and how to clear it. But the willpower and motivation to clear it well can be challenging from time to time. But when I confront it, it has a lasting impact.

A key to one's understanding of the importance of the environment may resonate more with where your occupation lies. I mean, how often do you hear of people stuck in jobs that they can't stand? This crushes the soul deeply and slowly. Because it's as if you are lying to yourself. But sometimes, we've no choice at the time because that is how our options are weighing on us; when this occurs, it's time to look tactfully at how you could make things better. First, realise what it is you actually enjoy doing. What could you do to earn an income that you feel you enjoy doing? When you do the things you love and enjoy at times, it doesn't feel like work. It's important to do things that are meaningful to us to maintain our own sanity and happiness.

When I cleared my environment, it gave me better peace of mind and calmness. My environment was affected very much by the people I was allowing into it. Things that I longed for in life began to flow to me more easily.

Full Moons

Well, well, well, here we are, and let me just check the day. It is 7 March, and it is a full moon now. I can't tell you if it's the new moon, but there's a full moon out there. Now, periodically, it is believed that the full moon symbolises new beginnings, endings, opportunities, and many more. For me, I feel like it is a new birthing of what is to come. While many opportunities are going to show their full face, I can't necessarily see it with my bare eyes, but I feel it in my heart. All my desires and dreams are manifesting, readjusting, and realigning in a way that will be unleashed in a manner that will be understandable to me through different patterns and signals throughout my life. I ask that they are obvious, so I'm ready to receive them.

Goals

OK, well, we all have goals and ambitions we strive to achieve. Even if you think you don't, my goals vary from being able to get out of bed. Being able to eat. Being able to get adequate sleep, being able to save, being able to grow as an individual, being a better parent, and being a better wife. And also trying to get a successful business on the ground, running successfully, and excelling in my work. Oh yeah, and also to be debt-free.

So, how do we achieve our own goals? I was trained to make my goals smart, but I changed them to have new meanings. We will go into that in the next chapter. Make sure they are specific to what you currently need in your life. It could be more time for yourself, more time for kids, to grow in work, or to improve your current health. But keep it simple, especially when starting out with your goals.

Are your goals measurable? It's important for the goals to be measurable so you can check in on how you're progressing. I can say from experience that this self-help guide and explorative journal have been the utmost help to me to this date. Sometimes, we get into the flow of things without realising that we are even in the flow of life. I set this goal to make a helpful tool that will benefit me and, hopefully, others. Suppose you are here right now at this moment. It means there is a segment of my process that's evident to have landed you here at this precise time of day. Secondly, I wanted to get a new job. I landed that new role and have passed my probation. Alongside that, I developed a further understanding of myself, my abilities, and the strength of character that is within me, especially when I adjusted my circle. I wanted to be a better me. This helps me see myself stop smoking with the strength of inner peace and also land a second job as part of my own personal development, which is also still a skill related to my current role. I wanted to become a better mother and wife. I now have better time management of how time is spent with my children, and I pretty much enjoy getting over their homework with them and giving them extra teaching lessons on areas they struggle with, along with supporting them in areas of their interests and being present to see that. A better wife, well, I guess we also get more time together, and life is more in harmony together as one that now my husband and I spend more time planning potential business ventures and adventures that we would long for. I also passed my driving test after numerous attempts, and I tell you, it felt so good. Somehow, the driving test felt so much harder than trying to obtain my degree. I've no idea.

But goals are ever-changing, depending on where you are in life. The trick is to never give up trying, but to be open to alternate routes and paths to get there. Never put so much pressure on yourself that it eats you up. We do eventually achieve what we want in life. It's very much the journey of getting to the goal where you learn the most. That left you thinking, well, what next? I'm done with this now. What do I do? We spend so much time trying to obtain a goal that we don't really take time to digest what we do once we get to where we want to get to.

Smart

Now, we're here in chapter SMART. I will tell you, it has taken me some time to buck the courage to even write in this chapter. Purely because I am referring back to what SMART goals are in achieving goals. But naturally, with my own twist to it.

When you think of the word smart, what are the first things that come to mind in terms of terminology? Is it, oh, that person knows it? The perceived intelligence of an individual that utilises their brain capacity in simplified ways. Those are what came to me in terms of terminology, and no, I really did not get to check on Google to see what Google comes up with as there is no reception underground. As you may have noticed throughout the course of this book, quite rightly so, it is an experience of one's own journeys and methods and simple guides of going from A to B, not to Z just yet, as that's quite a further distance, which will take more strategy time and practice to get there. As does each step that we generally take involve.

So, as a sports coach and business owner, one of the things you're taught is to devise a smart goal. Be it to help you plan how to start your business or how you plan to win a competition, you break them down section by section, then put them all together. So, my twist on it is the breakdown of SMART. It had been known to stand for:

S is for specific.

M is for measurable.

A is for achievable, R is for realistic, and T is for time.

Now, I would like you, in your own time, to write on a piece of paper all the S's that you can associate with yourself in order to devise your own SMART goal and why. So, my choices for myself would be specific, so I am focused on the specifics that I want to work on. Small so that I can work in small bursts of energy, but regularly. Strength so that I can endure the length of time to reach the goal and the tolerances.

M would again remain the same as measurable but with added management, maturity, motivation, mindfulness, and motherhood. I need management to oversee my tasks and duties. I will need maturity in taking ownership and accountability for my roles and actions. I will need motivation to keep going, and that means working through the days that I don't necessarily want to do anything. At times, those days are the very days that progress is unexpectedly at its best, as I guess you're walking blindly in faith that you can accomplish something. Mindfulness means that you are mindful of your thoughts and actions to get you through and in how you respond to your very own surroundings. We all have adverse effects on each other without realises that so does our environment. So be mindful of what works and what does not. But also, taking the time out for oneself to refocus will be beneficial in the long run. Motherhood—well, I am in this hood. At times, we can get engrossed in our own goals, depending on what they are, and they, too, could almost make you stray away from your responsibilities. I have said you need to choose words that resonate with you and your life, and we are all individuals. My goals are to be a better person, a better mother, and a better wife. When the first goal is achieved, all the others flow holistically. When I'm not at my best, the first thing that I lose is myself, and then everything else. That's the general process when you are no longer able to do things for yourself. It's thankful that I was able to love myself at a young age, even when just having the general difficulties of friendships. I was able to find love with my now-husband, so even when I'm down, I know they are still in good hands because they also got their father. It's important in life, from my experience, to have someone to love; it's like they are the other part of you, and you create a beautiful life. That is made up of each of you. If one is absent, you somehow still get that love of both through one. That's what is meant by marriage, as much as many also are for it, that you become one. So yes, motherhood is important for my SMART goal as it's part of my wholesomeness.

A's, as I'll repeat, are achievable, but as this one is achievable, I guess it is the most fitting place. To place that anything that you choose to change in life is achievable, even this simple task of adjusting a SMART goal to words that are suited to your own self is evidence of that. For me, achievable means, adjustment, attention, assertiveness, application, and appreciation. One of my goals due to traumatic experiences was to make sure that was my last time ever being sectioned. This is potentially achievable by making the necessary adjustments in life. Like kicking negative habits, be it substance abuse or unhealthy relationships. I've needed to pay careful attention to my life and what works and what doesn't. I had to be assertive with myself in my attitude towards life through careful application of the constant adjustments to putting myself in better situations; it reminds me to appreciate all that I have attained over time. Be kind about yourself of the changes you long to apply to yourself if you're not able to recognise the good things that you give to this life. Please try to find ways that can help you. Yes, at times, it helps to seek help from a counsellor or a confidante. Sometimes it's easier to find ways of expressing yourself without others. I find that works for me, as I just generally get to feeling so misunderstood often. So exercising, singing, creating a blend, or writing tend to work for me. In order to achieve anything in life, it is quite a deep journey that you must take with yourself.

R's for realistic, responsibility, respect, ranges, representation, repetition, rest, rarity, relationships, restoration, reasoning, and randomly. It is important that our SMART goals are, in fact, real and that they can be achieved. We do spend a lot of time in the virtual reality of life nowadays, and quite often, people are genuinely starting to forget and not actually recognise what is real. Responsibility is key to being responsible for your actions, choices, and decisions. Respect well. If you don't have any respect for yourself, how do you expect others to have respect for you? It goes a long way towards showing respect to others, regardless of who they are. Treat those as you would like to be treated, and that also means keeping yourself in check when things are going well and the ego tries to creep in, making you forget where you came from. Ranges well. Even for me, this is a unusual choice of words, but it is all in how you perceive life, the terminology, and the words you use. For me, I see more from a sportsman's eyes in that if I come at a specific angle or with a certain amount of speed, the range of the results can be varied. As can be your range of movement in which you are able to move your body. So, ranges are important for me with my SMART goals. Next, R is representation. It often takes me time to return to the base of what I represent within my endeavours. I can be my own worst enemy and harshest critic. I tend to believe that I represent my sense of self. That's why I find the definitions of our names to be so important. When I started on my venture with Letitia Antoinette, it took me back to, oh, I want to wear my own name instead of other brands. I'd like for others to see my name as a household name. But mainly, it was about how I felt, like my name has meaning; it means to bring joy beyond praise. If I can live my life bringing that to my life, then maybe if others wear something with my name attached to it, somehow they will experience their own joy beyond praise in their own way. I am a representation of purpose and of the truth of what is true to me. What may be true for me, I guess, may not be true for you, but it's our experiences and conditions that allow us to view the way we do. So one of the things I noticed when I was in the process of growing was that the attitude amongst some ambassadors had changed to feel like competition. There is always competition in life, and in business, this was not my purpose or what I represented. I wanted to inspire others to find their own joys in their lives beyond praise by purely believing in their own abilities. Not always are we destined to be amongst people the whole journey, some just partially as a guide to get them over a hurdle or to the next step that they were already so close to. So, I changed the focus of my business back to myself. I am the key asset to getting it running. Repetition is part of the process. When things get up and running; it's going to be repetitive. Some can struggle with repetition, as it can become boring. I think it can be a natural battle of ADHD and bipolar that the attention wants to flee, so try not to overthink what needs doing. Rest can be good, and too much rest can lead down the slope of depression, so adequate rest from work, interaction, TV, and social media can be very healthy in restoring one's mind. Relationships are important when growing and developing. It's important to have a healthy relationship with yourself and then others, or you spend too much time sabotaging any potential successes. Well, restoration is all that this book is about: restoring oneself to a stronger version of yourself. It is included as part of the importance of my smart goal because it does take being reset to restore. Think of yourself strangely enough as a computer. If there is a virus or some kind of malfunction, it sure saves you a lot of money without the need for a specialist when you know how to restore a device yourself. I've had to be restored many times with my hospitalisations and make use of all the available specialists to get back to functioning at my best potential. I believe that at thirty-three, I'm in the flow of things. Reasoning is every other way of explaining why, how, and what makes you do, but coming to an understanding of all those aspects as one. It's healthy to have reasonings for the actions and choices we make to propel ourselves. I really want you to choose the words that best represent your own sense of meaningfulness, so this smart plan is as true and effective as possible for you. And last but not least, my R's are random. We, in a sense, are one day randomly here as much as, in the most cases, nine months to be born. I tend to have a preference for things randomly occurring; planning is not always the best for me. And feelings are as random as they come. I've had to assume my business on randomness based on my personality and behaviour and also in stating that I'm the niche of my business as there's only one me. I'm unique to who I am, so to how I do things, being randomly choosen is also key in knowing how my own system and processes work and materialise, so unpredictability is a virtue and a part of my own adventure.

Last but not least, we arrive at T. I think I've spent so much time just justifying my choices of adaptations to my SMART goal that I feel the time has already shown itself. The other T's are trust and truth. I have to trust my process and myself, but always be true. That admits when things are going well and not so well, too.

Accomplishments

So often, we don't even recognise our own accomplishments. People are generally quick to talk about the degrees they got from the reputable companies they've been associated with. It straight-up feels like a means of exclusion.

I like to keep my accomplishments basic and simple. I believe they vary depending on how we view life and how we have experienced life up to now. This year, my accomplishment was landing a full-time job in a field that I trained in as soon as I became a mother. My further accomplishment in myself was the ability to change to a new regime and routine, which I am currently maintaining and improving. My further accomplishments are my two sons; they are happy and healthy, and both are in education. Another accomplishment is going into my eleventh year of marriage with my husband. Another is not being hospitalised and loving with a renewed health and sense of wellbeing.

Accomplishments are not limited or restrictive. But purely on what we say they are to us. It does not take approval from others to accomplish something. But approval to oneself of the reality of what you have overcome in your day-to-day. I mean, even the ability to try is something, as is getting out of bed to face the day.

Sometimes, we forget to talk encouragingly and lovingly to ourselves, and it can make all the difference. How often do you take the time out of your day to recognise what you have accomplished?

Pitch

It might sound crazy, but, hoorah, I'll go for it. The whole importance of this book is for you to kinda in a nutshell transform and restore yourself. Just as you see, you have been journeying with me in my own process if you are now here at the pitch.

Quite often, in business and generally in life, we have to pitch ourselves. As to why we are so great for a job, our ideas are great to be invested in. Why am I the best person to get into a relationship with, involve yourself with, collaborate with, have a friendship with, etc.? I hope you get the gist.

Have you ever pitched to yourself? Why are you the best person in your life? Can you proudly get in front of the mirror right now and state, what's so good about you? We are all great, and little too often do we stray away from understanding how great we are. We drive away and compare our efforts to what others are doing and what someone else is achieving. I want you to convince yourself confidently. Why you deserve to live the best life you long for and what skills and attributes you have can make a difference.

I'll give it a go with you here right now. My name is Duchess Letitia. I'm a proud mother of two. I deserve the best in my life because each day is a gift. I've been gifted to be able to create children. The love I was given as a child helped, guided, and shaped me into the mother and wife I am today. My grit and hard work give me the life that I have. My determination will help see me through to better days and more success. My supportive husband, through ten years of marriage and fifteen years together, is my best friend and soul mate. It takes dedication and sacrifice to get a family unit working and flowing. Through any obstacles we may face, it makes us stronger. I may have disabilities that do not define me. If I work hard, believe in myself, and listen to my heart and my intuition, I can achieve all that I want. I never give up because I'm a strong force of energy that is destined for great things. I already have many of those great things with the love that has endured within and the many gifted talents I've been blessed with. So I'm the best person to be me, and it shall stay that way.

I think that was quite a strange task, but hey, give it ago. What's your pitch to you? I'd love to find out. Please feel free to share your pitches with me about why you're the best person to live your life for you. So often, some people think they know you better than you. It is a saying that many do say. Quite often, we forget exactly who we are.

Now, if you can pitch yourself to how great you are, from having gone through goals and smarts, you might be able to break down how you go pitching for other opportunities out there that you long for.

I say I am the best person to fulfil the roles that come available because I believe I am capable of great things abundantly through all adversity. I seek to understand, improve, and enhance my skills so I can always be the best at what I do. I am the change.

Growing Pains

Quite often, I express my difficulties being in pain. It's in the lower half of my body that I notice the most heavy legs, numb legs, and a loss of ability to move them for a while. But what if we looked at these physical pains differently? In a more metaphysical way. Maybe that pain in the legs is etherically a cacoon trying to wrap up around you as a sheet of protection. Because even though experiencing the pain for some can be temporary, a few hours, days, months, weeks, years, goodness, we definitely don't want years. But the cacoon is wrapping over the legs, and the medication is taking effect to allow the head to rest first, then the pain. *What if you could connect with the understanding of the process that the caterpillar and butterfly experience? Maybe it's partly a healing crisis working through your body, or you transferred energy from the contact of others who have been ill, and through your body, you're experiencing it. But yet something great is about to be borne from this as you rest, recover, restore strength, and emerge.* It's just a thought.

Pain fuels the character of who I'm becoming; through the endurance of resilience, I connect with the traumas my ancestors overcame. They guide and walk with me, trying to keep me upright so I can keep fighting to live life the best I can. But to also enable the fact that it takes time to heal.

In my healing, there are a lot of internal lives that one must understand. Purely those internal lives being the very DNA that runs inside somewhere, somehow there is a sequence formed of the emotive feelings that we feel. I will question myself endlessly, argue with myself endlessly, criticise, and occasionally talk about the good things I've been able to achieve and accomplish myself. I recently cut ties with a circle that I felt was socially excluding me in order to stop feeling that feeling, which just meant stepping away and not engaging. That means I simply put a block on my social media or numbers as a means of stepping away. It sounds pathetic, but so much drama comes from these things nowadays. Then I noticed the members of the circle liking my posts, considering I had blocked them from a social media platform, making me realise that I hadn't blocked them from all. I've experienced stalking in my lifetime. Social media just makes that an all-so-easy thing to achieve nowadays. So, yeah, I get to try to run to not be seen, but yet a big part of my work requires me to be seen, especially when it comes to the entrepreneurship of selling your own products. They haven't called me names or insulted me; they just unintentionally at times let me out. So my way to deal with that was, like I said, to step away and be unavailable. It is a means of pushing people further away who do not know how to be close to you. I think that that can also be a learning curve for multiculturalism in England in general. So many different cultures have a different understanding of social norms that are the norm for them. That difference in ways can be easily understood.

Self-Realisation

Self-realisation is the understanding and full development of oneself and your talent and abilities. Now, as much as it is a great place to reach, it is also an eye-opener. It does not mean you are perfect for having reached self-realisation; more so, imperfectly perfect to you for who you are.

As the individual I am, I know I've been gifted with being that jack of all trades, so to speak. I guess that makes sense as to why I do so many different things and also have my hands in as many pies as possible. It's my own natural nature, be it that it's even related to my star sign and characteristics. Being aware of these things enables me to be able to utilise my different skills and abilities to the best of my own capability. That is not to say that everything I put my hands on is going to be a success, because that can be one of the disadvantages when you are good at many things. There are aspects that are neglected that hinder failure in certain areas.

An example would be when I first started my makeup line with one product that sold out, but because that experience was successful, I jumped the gun and decided to expand quicker instead of gradually. Then I was just left with so much stock, unable to sell. I diluted the ratio of success so much that I then couldn't put the marketing effort equally across all products consistently and then neglected the main product that was a success. It's a learning curve, and generally, in development, each step is vital to enabling sustainability across the board.

I've noticed I always like to try new things or be involved with projects, and my mind wanders to what else I can do. Yet it's achievable when the projects come to me naturally rather than when I seek them out. When I seek them out, I become flabbergasted because I've then lost count of how many different opportunities I've been trying to attach myself to.

My frustrations are my ability to read things for what they truly are, regardless of how painful the truth is, and not actually respond. But only when I feel I can or should. A part of me can see the true faces of others when they truly detest something about me and choose not to say anything. Instead, I tolerate them until they actually come forth and show their hand, even though one may know their hand already. I'm not sure if it means to be better and safer to know for sure that my senses were right. Instead of being seen as acting out impulsively by cutting ties, or that I view negatively and shouldn't think that way. But nine out of ten, I usually spot the overall vibe. Even then, I try to view the best possible outcomes of the hurt I'm going to go through. My answer is if it can be avoided at all costs, then avoid it by all means necessary. I think that is why there is a big part of me that genuinely prefers lonely. It is not at all loneliness. But peacefulness. Some people like to exaggerate how long they're been together. The reason those times have generally survived is purely due to the naturally long absences in each other's lives. Too much of anything can feel suffocating, controlling, and invasive; those are traits that make you feel obsessive and possessive, which is just not healthy. The perpetrators of those types of traits naturally see themselves as protective and lack the capacity to actually be able to view the way they behave. I've had to learn that the hard way. So, I no longer allow myself to, in a sense, build such kinds of connections. When I finally discover that such connections have been built, I release them as swiftly as possible; there needs to be an explanation. You come to your own understanding in life through experiences, and not everything comes with explanations. You find those answers on your own as life goes with you.

I am my own worst enemy, and I'll embrace my own miseries. I don't like to share those miseries, but I will sit them myself and become my own frenemy till I overcome them myself. I'm not a person who likes people unexpectedly around them. Highly distrusting of people, as it's just human nature to hurt each other as much as it is to love one another. To me, hurt comes from hate, so once I've experienced the hurt of others, there is a big part of me that completely forgives and moves on. Don't forget, so you can't be near it.

I can't say my responses are among the healthiest, but it makes all the difference to be knowledgeable of who one is and how different situations and timelines garner reactions over different durations of time. I can reflect upon the words that I've written and the responses I've seen to either see them as a great surprise that I felt or view them the way I do. It means that you don't truly know how anyone feels until they say something, but even then, anyone can try to lie with what they say or not.

I, with my ways, can be viewed as strange, selfish, insensitive, blunt, lazy, and rude; listing any more than that would just be tearing oneself down too far. I've always been a misunderstood person. It is not anything that I'm striving to change any more than my protection of myself. But you're just as vulnerable in your misunderstandings as if you understood. So, I guess the strangeness of the viewings comes from not being understood.

Certain habits, good or bad, occur depending on how rested I've been. Am I too hasty and too quick to cut ties? Naturally, there is a part that has to say that I'm not. My autism makes it difficult to express verbally to some people how I feel. Purely because I don't know how to do so in a way that won't feel offensive from my experiences. So, quite often, I guess I run because their ways feel strange and insulting to me.

Sagittarian

Now, my understanding of what is known about Sagittarians is that we are among the most hated star signs of the zodiac. Viewed as among the weirdest, most difficult, kinda crazy, and misunderstood signs. Now, I thought this was all part of self-realisation, reflection, etc. Until I was pondering my thoughts, like what hold up? You actually get along, and then you don't get along with specific star signs. Maybe that's the correlating relationship between all things black and white. Not necessarily just, how can I say it, mental health per say.

So apparently, fire signs don't get along with earth signs that much, and the irony of that is that my biggest falls out with individuals of my past kinda still present are Taurus, Virgo, and Capricorn. But I've always found that star signs and the relations and correlations are merely guidance for possibilities, not necessarily set in stone.

I believe I am free-spirited and witted. I do love with all my heart, and sometimes it is as if I can visualise rays of light oozing out of me, dispersing to all my loved ones or people in my life and those who have passed through. I take my time to understand that, oh yeah, maybe then, at that time, we weren't meant to be amongst each other for each other's growth. But yet, experience is needed to enable growth. I literally love everyone. I love being around people and learning about other people's journeys, experiences, and hopes and dreams. It lifts me up to want to make the most of life. But yet, my everyday battles are my own in how I internalise the world around me. How I digest the information in this whole process of expression and writing has been such an experience of speaking clarity into my life. You know, sometimes my abruptness comes to completely the wrong way. Sometimes, my open-heartedness is just asking for trouble to allow my heart to be stamped on. But it is a way that I learn. Through vulnerability and pain. There is nothing like wearing your heart on your sleeve. But you know when you are able to step away from your egotistical self and see how your own mind is viewing and perceiving everything. And try looking beyond to perhaps understand what the message is that God the Universe is trying to relay to you. You might begin to notice—oh yeah, there is a pattern. Well, let me change that right here because we are given a choice to be able to adjust, adapt, and change. Hence, throughout this book, I asked for you all to devise your own strategized SMART goal of what they mean specifically to you and your life.

All throughout this self-restoration process, I've been longing to be better. To be a better mother is to be a better wife, a better sister, a better daughter, and a better friend. Life takes us on ups and downs and runs around a… How we understand what we are going through comes with time and wisdom. So yes, Sagittarians can come across as messy in their ways, but understand that I do not speak as a representative for all but for myself of the traits that I am aware of. So, our messy ways, as for most, I believe, make sense to us in how we function. Adventure is key in our lifetimes. I'm not sure that we are completely stuck on one specific job, but when we are, it has to have a multitude of many different skills or be right up our alley of our many joys of self. Creativity is our heart's middle name. We like things to be innovative, and it's quite exciting to learn new ways and create different things, even more so if they have not been done before. That is an added bonus. We lead and challenge ourselves, and we will crazily place ourselves in the deep end when not knowing how to swim as a means of fast-tracking our skills to be able to do so. I spent a lot of my young days physically doing that, going into the deep end believing I'm a mermaid and coming straight up. I can't really swim, but I could swim a few metres or so, and that was great for me. I've kind of carried that experience throughout my life. I feel I do make a great leader and a difference in others' lives. It is just that I get so engrossed in my work and what I will be doing that I do not actually realise that I'm making any kind of difference. It is always with love, so it just feels like breathing, and you go with the flow. It is when you are consciously aware that you are good at this that you may panic, which usually occurs to me, that I run away.

Self-Doubt

I think there comes a point when many of us may talk without thinking. Act without thinking and just realise, after the time has passed or during the actual time, what they are exactly doing. It happens; it is the norms of reality for how we as beings behave.

What I'd like to get to the bottom of is: how do we persist in moving on with life? How do we move forward? How do we let go of the past? The simplest analogies, I believe, are to not think of the past, not dwell on it, and try to be with the vibes and flow of things that seem to be serving your spirit well.

It's not that difficult to trust yourself and your abilities when you give yourself the chance to. It has a lot to do with mindsets and belief systems. These are, at times, affected by your own experiences, which have set conditions for you. Which, therefore, limits you to being able to see only so far. If at all, the ability to see.

There is so much magic, power, light, love, and beauty just in the very core of you. I wish that you would be able to see how amazing you are and exactly how far you have come in life. Too often, we are quick to ignore our efforts, criticise, and doubt. This isn't for everyone, but bad days come and bad days go. Do you resonate with your soul's purpose? Were you put here to fulfil something in your life? Have you done that? Are you doing that? How does that feel? Or are you still figuring out who you are? It is also natural not to have any of these answers because we are ever-changing in life. You're not necessarily the same every year. Life grows on us. The importance is being able to see goodness and being able to be positive. But then again, everyone is different in what is perceived as a good life. Happiness isn't necessarily the aim of life for some. The reality of the world is that good and bad do exist. Some be evil, some be love. Darkness brings the negative emotiveness of feelings and lightens the positive. Ideally, balance is key to maintaining harmony.

I quite often go through my own means of self-doubt. My way of combating that is to dare myself to do things that take me out of my comfort zone as a means to shut down the negative self-talk to myself of doubt. Many of us do this to ourselves. That's why I mentioned above what your purpose is. What were you brought here to do? Even self-doubt is part of the journey of how you overcome your own internal demons. When you learn to pay no mind to self-doubt and learn to teach yourself a positive dialogue, you will notice great changes just by activating the power of your mind and truly connecting within. Things fall into place quicker, and efforts seem effortless. Even though there may have been chatter in the mind, but the chatter in the spirit stands stronger than the unseen, which helps you keep things together.

So, move forward with faith and strength. Can you let go of what just happened, even five minutes ago, and focus on where you are exactly right now? This is what matters: the present and what we can do with our present time to get to our future selves. So learn to be more clearly headed; try to ease worries and doubts. Be patient with your progress and your efforts. Because what may not seem like much effort to you now, you will look back and recognise how much it took to keep going.

Your Last Day

Now, it may seem a bit extreme as a means to kick sense into you. But most of us take the days we are given for advantage, as much as we may deny it. I spend my Mondays through Fridays carrying out treatments for patients battling cancer. No date is guaranteed for anyone. Sometimes, we don't learn from lessons; sometimes, life gives us the greatest battles through the conditions we are faced with and different situations. But what happens when you know exactly how much time you have left? I recently returned to the state of health I was in earlier in the year as a non-smoker. I went back to smoking, and then, after having a health assessment, I soon stopped smoking. The results of my lung function test were enough to make me stop automatically, as I do want to live a long life with fewer health complications. If you were given your last day on earth, what would you do?

Now, this is not just a question for you but also for myself. I want this book to be a tool to get you back on track. Insight into how one gets themselves back on track while also always beating themselves down. Finishing and leaving you all with a fast track to getting yourself on par. What if all you've been experiencing has led you here to help you find your answers? Let me guide you the best I can. First things first. This is the last day of Monday. Now, how does Monday go?

Monday goes just the same as any other day, be it Tuesday, Wednesday, Thursday, Friday, Saturday, or Sunday. So, there are no correlations between which day or date is the deciding factor in what you do. I have a sense we should naturally take each day as it is the last, as each day isn't promised. Some die in their sleep, not knowing that they will be there ever after. Some relationships can suddenly be the last without any warning, causing such destruction, hurt, and pain. Like, was anyone ever prepared for things to end? When a life ends, it ends. When a situation ends, it ends. When dinner is finished, it ends. One could argue that well, my spirit and my soul endure forever more once the body dies. When the relationship ends, maybe that physical part of seeing each other stops, but that is not to say that the memory of what it was will just fade and disappear. When that meal ends, it's not to say the food completely disappears. It is transported inside, releasing its nutritional benefits to the body and serving hunger. When a situation ends, there are lasting effects of what was and what could or should have been. Are our endings not purely beginnings? Somehow, we all leave an essence, a presence of our being amongst others. Everything in life has its own existential purpose that is not always known to everyone but is always understood by ourselves over time. It doesn't make much sense to forever spend time trying to know what that purpose is, but to do what is needed from that calling you and urgency within you. Everything is connected in a strange metaphysical way. You could spend a lifetime just trying to figure out exactly how that is; we are here to enjoy the journeys that we have devised and planted within ourselves. Just how well do you or will you water your own seed with goodness to ensure that the growth is continual and forever blooming in the life that has been designed for you?

    I named this the last day because this is the last day that I'm here with you to share my story. But even though I chose this day to be the last day to write to you, when will the last day be for you to be here with me? We transcended together across time to get here. How shall you reach out in your life to yourself and to those who mean the dearest and truest of love to you? If you don't know how to, do you know now? Please do not waste a single day again not sharing your love and how you feel with those you care about. We all matter, and so do you. I ask that you love yourself a little bit more and share your light and gifts with all of us because you made a difference and lit up my day. Spread your wings and be imperfectly perfect as you are. Namaste

Emergency Passport

An emergency passport is not exactly what you may think it is. But then again, for me, it is exactly as it sounds: an emergency passport, which is something to be used in an emergency but with quick access to transportation. This book, as I'll repeat, is about restoration, understanding the processes of those low dips, and trying to rise out of them. Exploring the thought processes and how one's mind badgers them all at the same time. Now, I don't believe it is a system that is used in all areas. Nonetheless, when you have gone through such experiences as mine through hospitalisations, otherwise known as sectioned for mental health, some of the recovery road processes connect and link you to a wide range of different external services to help sustain your health and well-being. I fell under the north locality team. I was always eager to gain as many tools as possible that would naturally allow me to maintain my mental health as an alternative to orthodox medication. Mainly to do with one, the medication tended to give me new symptoms, making me less independent. I felt worse and was scared of whatever the side effects would be. It felt like a lifetime of battling with doctors and trying to justify my reasons that these side effects aren't healthy.

The irony and frustration of those experiences were obviously that the doctors were well aware of what the potential side effects of the medication would be beforehand. The fact was, they only knew once a patient had tried it to what extent the effects would be. Hence, there is such a wide array of different medications to trial. I know they say buying drugs from people is terrible, but the medications I get from the doctors leave me higher than any street drug. I only ever touched cannabis, which I believe is still effective for chronic illnesses. It is all about the safety and reliability of where the production of the plant has taken place and its effects. I ended up with strains that had been laced with all kinds, hence my side effects. But nonetheless, yes. Let's get back to the emergency passport.

So, an emergency passport helps those who are diagnosed with mental health be cared for in a particular way. Now, it was later discovered after self-studying myself for many years that I have other mental health conditions alongside bipolar affective disorder; I think that is also a major factor in why medication hasn't been fully successful for my mental health. So basically, with bipolar, I go into a hyperstate known as mania. But the mania process very much feels like the nesting phase expectant mothers go through when they know their baby is due to come in a matter of days. Your body naturally gets a sense of spiritual intuition; it's time to prepare. Now, consciously and unconsciously, I sensed that something was coming in my life that I was unaware of spiritually. My first ever episode occurred weeks after taking medication for mental health and months after having my baby. I never had a natural birth until my second born. It is natural for the body to go low into a state of depression, and it's also natural to be able to drive out of that phase of depression over time. I believe I disturbed the natural process of that through the use of medication, and my body responded in shock and crisis because it was being synthetically forced to feel good.

I started to cleanse my body through fasting. It went on for about a week. I would perhaps one night sleep five hours, then the next night four hours to three to two to one to twenty minutes, if that. I nibble on only fruit and nuts throughout the remaining days and water throughout, plus supplements. I had immense strength and energy during this time. It was like the less I slept, the stronger and more energy I had. My abilities grew because anxieties and fear of capabilities disappeared. I was doing a lot of ballet throughout my house; I was extra flexible. I constantly heard music throughout the day. I couldn't stop dancing, and I couldn't stop singing. I journeyed to the inner child of fun and play that I became to spend my days playing fancy dress up. My fancy dress-up saw me getting out my wedding dresses, my pageant dresses, my handbags, and my heels. Testing out different wigs with different outfits and then cat-walking around the house. Every surreal moment I had experienced in my life, somehow I had to connect with them through simple activities like wearing the outfits and cat walking and dancing. I was overwhelmed with happiness and elevation. But the moment anyone wanted to try to put a hold on or stop those amazing moments in my world at that time, it released a dark switch. I become defensive, trying to throw my shoes at my husband.

Wanting to recklessly and carelessly do shopping for God knows what. Something inside just made me feel like I had to do this. I swear, down, I felt like there was some magnetised thread pulling me around, so I was drawn to different things. I came to a point where I even felt like Jesus was walking through me. It is, really. What you see in front of your eyes is, although you hear it, a completely different narrative of the events occurring.

The truth of the matter is that, over time, I experimented with so many different medications. My hospitalisations came as a result of the medication trying to get completely out of my system. Lack of sleep, overstress, and laced marijuana. It takes an accrued period of time to get to that state. You know, the very first time I ever went, I thought it was a joke. The last few became wake-up calls. However, I was always trying to get the chance to implement my emergency passport plan to prevent hospitalisation. It nearly occurred. The prevention key process is adamant and vital, but it takes years to understand what on earth is going on. I tried to get my spouse to pass me this medication, etc., but the need was to be outdoors to dance and shake off the extra energy to tire oneself out. But we couldn't get there because of the fear of not being able to contain what was going on while also managing to keep an eye on the children. So, you know, when that fails, the best place is hospitalisation. However, after the final hospitalisation, I never felt like I had worked so much. I was there to sort myself out at the same time and support the staff on duty, as they didn't know how to handle some of the patients, especially those who were talking about different religious things. Somehow, I was able to calm them. Calming them eased me. Because I was back to doing what I enjoy and do best: helping support others.

Music in Spirit

Well, well, well. It does surprise me to be here at this chapter so late in the book. I actually can't believe that I hadn't consciously thought to even write a section on music. It was thanks to my brother Derick in Sacramento that I re-evaluated what I had written about. He asked me to collaborate with him on a poem. Then I started badgering my brain with questions on music, disabilities, and how I lead my followers. I was like, hmm, interesting now he hasn't just randomly called me at eight fifteen a.m. English time when God knows what time it is when he is out of the blue for no reason. His call came just as I had written a post online about how the journey of this book has been lifting me. Then he reminded me of our musical journey, as we do have a few songs on which we have collaborated together. So, I'm here to share.

I've always loved music, and I still do. It heals my wounded heart and soothes my gentle soul. I remember when I was younger we used to do family dance offs at family get togethers. To see who was the best dancer I recall always winning I believe. Go to community centres came close first, with my brother dancing to Will Smith, getting jiggy with it, and also being part of dance clubs.

Music in spirit is the force with which one moves to me. My connection with music came from listening to hymns in church and choreographing my own dance routine in a nativity play at the age of five as the Star. I just remember the silence of the audience, the flashing lights of cameras at the end of the dance, and the applause. I don't believe you truly understand what is really going on at that age physically. You feel very much more of what feels good in your heart. But I knew from a young age that I never wanted to be with the crowd of angels protecting baby Jesus. More so, the star that leads the path does its own thing. That way of thinking has remained with me throughout the duration of my life today. I guess without realising it, I very much prefer things that way; it means fewer complications. But endurance of one's own complexities of life to deal with.

From age seven, I got to do more within the creative arts. We had school plays and outside agencies coming in to teach after-school activities. Whenever it came to a performance that was a serious role for me, I put my whole heart into that. I became a different character. My funniest one to play was Lady Macbeth. The outfit I got to wear was fantastic. The classic line I can recall is that the deed is done with a wicked, snide laugh. Somehow, I had a natural flair for playing naughty characters. I enjoyed being one of the orphans in Annie. I was given two words to sing. That matters when playing Beth. And all that mattered to me was to have the chance for my voice to be heard. But the words that were sung that mattered were everything. I recall my music teacher, Miss Bavister at the time, saying how I had such a powerful voice. To this day, when people generally say you've such a powerful voice, I always thought it meant in terms of the strength of how it sounded. Like, you know how strength sounds? Do you know what I mean? But then I realised I think they mean how deep your sound reaches through to a person. Over time, as an artist, I've seen people cry from listening to my voice in the way that I have sung. Fans messaged me, telling me how my song saved their souls. For me, that power is the most frustrating thing at times. I'm oblivious to understanding exactly how I had that effect. Or why are they responding this way? Power at times is also not knowing how powerful and impactful you are. It is almost as though there is a dissociation or detachment from what I do. Because it's all God, not me. But in the religion that I was raised in, Roman Catholicism, It's often said through him, with him in him.

Spiritually speaking, I believe God uses us all. I am but a servant, making use of my gifts, which reach out to others. So, I assume there is part of me that is connectedly listening to my purpose in how to use it without realising that it is.

Music has been a great medicine for me throughout my life. I began writing at the age of twelve, sitting in an English class. This was the age when I began to recognise that there was something different in me. Or that something was just changing in me. My connections with others were changing, and I felt more lost within myself. I believe that I kinda felt left behind in the trends or know-how of what occurs at that age. Writing became my friend and my way of listening to what is in my heart. My way of being able to express how I felt without needing to hear anyone's opinions on what it was that I was feeling. My first song was Open Your Eyes. The words that came to me were:

> This world isn't all what it seems to you.
> You wouldn't believe all the things you knew.
> Don't think that I'm tryna lie to you.
> It's true it's true it's true.
> There's too much suffering and too much dying.
> Big cheats lie and murderers are set free.
> There's not enough company for you and me cause there's too much suffering and dying.
> Lying and crying
> Open your eyes and see.
> I'm walking down the streets, which isn't very neat.
> I'm hearing shouting and swearing to
> Why are we the way we are?
> Why do we shout at our dads and ma?
> They brought us into this world.
> Look how we treat them; this just ain't right.
> Everything's so uptight, and I can't bare the sight.
> I don't know what is happening, but it's happening to you I don't know what is happening buts it's happening to you.
> It's true it's true it's true.
> Open your eyes and see.

So yeah, I used this song to feature in my final drama play the *Mad World* instrumental as a monologue. Towards the end of high school, I even managed to get tears in my eyes. My final drama piece was based on a young lady trying to decide whether to keep her child and all the emotions she was going to face from those around her. I directed that play and was quite proud of it. I got to make use of writing in different contexts while performing together with the written piece.

Little did I know that I would go on to live a career involved in the creative arts. I still write songs to this day, and it's a work in progress for my visual works, but mostly that has been shown through my music video directing and set designs. Music is a medicine to me that, when abused, it's like that's all I can see. It helps me express my innermost feelings. When there is a lack of music, I can feel lost or deflated. Too much can feel so addictive that I can't stop. So music has been important to me but has to be used in moderation.